▶ ESSENTIAL SURVIVAL STORIES

DESERT
SURVIVAL STORIES

BY ALEXIS BURLING

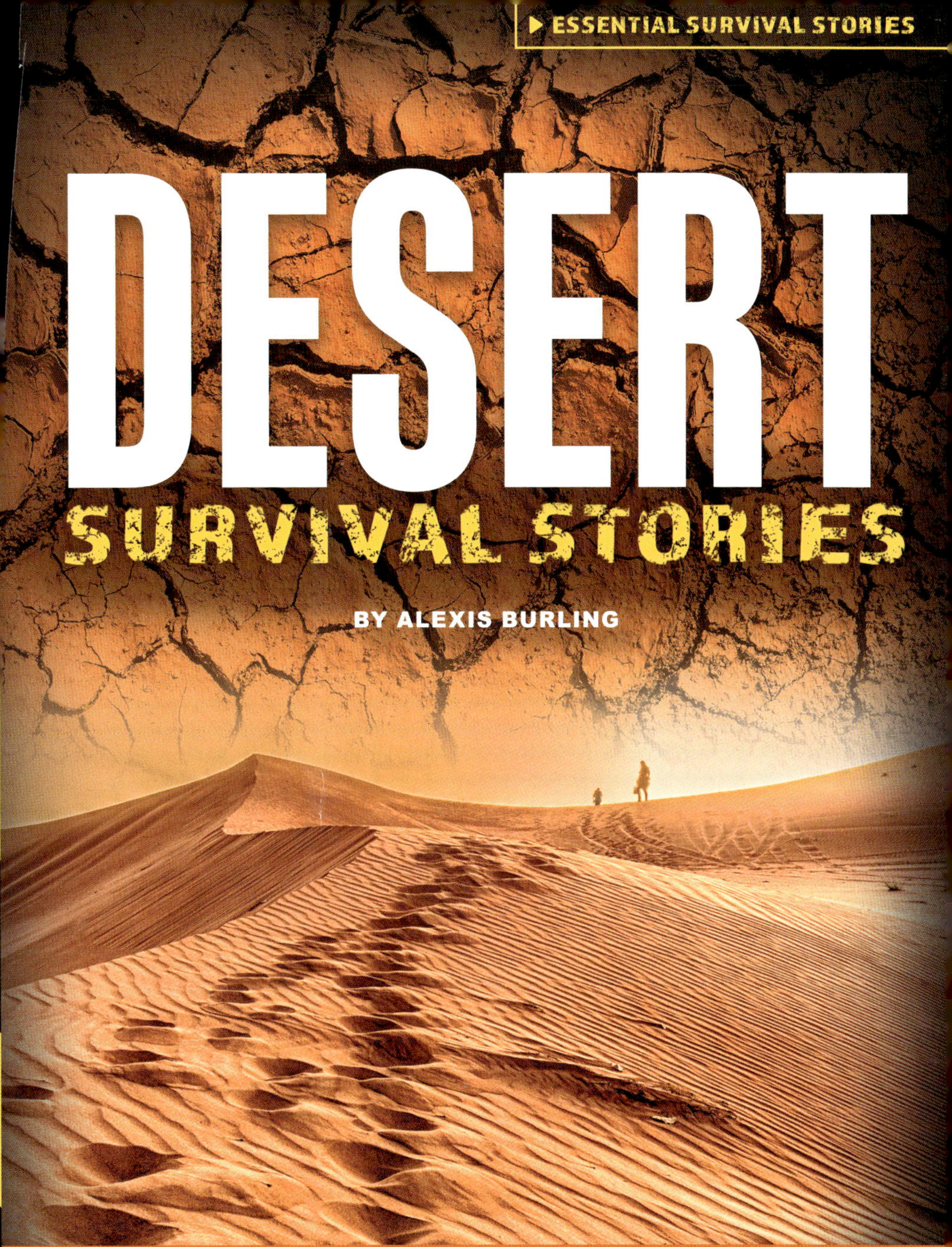

Essential Library

An Imprint of Abdo Publishing
abdobooks.com

ABDOBOOKS.COM

Published by Abdo Publishing, a division of ABDO, PO Box 398166, Minneapolis, Minnesota 55439. Copyright © 2024 by Abdo Consulting Group, Inc. International copyrights reserved in all countries. No part of this book may be reproduced in any form without written permission from the publisher. Essential Library™ is a trademark and logo of Abdo Publishing.

Printed in the United States of America, North Mankato, Minnesota.
102023
012024

THIS BOOK CONTAINS RECYCLED MATERIALS

Cover Photo: Wessam Noufal/Shutterstock Images
Interior Photos: Wessam Noufal/Shutterstock Images, 1; Kamil Zelezik/Shutterstock Images, 4–5; Robb Hannawacker/National Park Service, 6–7; Shutterstock Images, 8, 20, 50–51, 66, 77, 80, 84–85, 89 (backpack, sunglasses, knife, first aid), 89 (boots, food), 89 (sunscreen), 89 (GPS); CB Travel/Shutterstock Images, 11, 32–33; Joshua Resnick/Shutterstock Images, 13, 87; Eniko Balogh/Shutterstock Images, 16–17; Robert Mcgillivray/Shutterstock Images, 22; Kleber Cordeiro/Shutterstock Images, 25; Hannah Schwalbe/National Park Service, 28–29; Richard Stephen/Shutterstock Images, 35; Erik Sampers/Abaca Press/Sipa USA/AP Images, 38–39, 44–45, 47; Jean-Philippe Ksiazek/AFP/Getty Images, 41; Anatoliy Lukich/Shutterstock Images, 53; Ivanova Ksenia/Shutterstock Images, 54; Gary C. Tognoni/Shutterstock Images, 59; Kurt Moses/National Park Service, 60; Whit Richardson/Alamy, 62; Whit Richardson/Stockimo/Alamy, 69; Robert Crum/Shutterstock Images, 73; Steven Giles/Shutterstock Images, 74–75; Benny Marty/Shutterstock Images, 79; Creative Studio/Shutterstock Images, 89 (hat); iStockphoto, 89 (map); Walter Otto/Shutterstock Images, 89 (water bottle); Brian Goodman/Shutterstock Images, 93; Mark Skalny/Shutterstock Images, 96–97; Jim David/Shutterstock Images, 99

Editor: Marie Pearson
Series Designer: Maggie Villaume

Library of Congress Control Number: 2023939437

PUBLISHER'S CATALOGING-IN-PUBLICATION DATA

Names: Burling, Alexis, author.
Title: Desert survival stories / by Alexis Burling
Description: Minneapolis, Minnesota: Abdo Publishing, 2024 | Series: Essential survival stories | Includes online resources and index.
Identifiers: ISBN 9781098292195 (lib. bdg.) | ISBN 9798384910138 (ebook)
Subjects: LCSH: Survival--Juvenile literature. | Adventure and adventurers--Juvenile literature. | Desert survival--Juvenile literature. | Hot weather conditions--Juvenile literature. | Wilderness survival--Juvenile literature.
Classification: DDC 613.69--dc23

CONTENTS

CHAPTER ONE
A TERRIFYING FALL 4

CHAPTER TWO
THE DANGERS OF THE DESERT 16

CHAPTER THREE
CLAIRE IS FOUND 28

CHAPTER FOUR
THE RACE TO NOWHERE 38

CHAPTER FIVE
A ROAD TRIP GONE WRONG 50

CHAPTER SIX
TAZ TO THE RESCUE 62

CHAPTER SEVEN
TRAPPED IN THE OUTBACK 74

CHAPTER EIGHT
SURVIVING THE DESERT 84

ESSENTIAL FACTS 100
GLOSSARY 102
ADDITIONAL RESOURCES 104
SOURCE NOTES 106
INDEX 110
ABOUT THE AUTHOR 112

CHAPTER 1

A TERRIFYING FALL

It was a gorgeous spring day on May 22, 2018, and 36-year-old New Zealand writer Claire Nelson was feeling restless. She was house-sitting for her friends Natalie and Lou for a few weeks while they were away and to take a break from her hectic life as a journalist. Their house was near Palm Springs, California. She had been working nonstop in London, England, and then in Toronto, Canada. More than anything, she wanted to find some peace, quiet, and time away from the computer.

Ever since she moved to London in her twenties, Nelson had gone hiking or camping whenever she needed to relax. Sometimes she went with friends or

◀ Palm Springs is a desert city at the foot of Mount San Jacinto.

family members. Other times, especially when she got older and acquired more skills, she went alone. Being among the towering trees made her feel a part of something larger. She found it helped clear her head and made her feel calm and at peace.

On that May day, Nelson decided to go for a hike in Joshua Tree National Park. The park is a huge protected area in Southern California. It's full of craggy rocks and the large, spiky treelike plants that give the park its name. Nelson had heard about the park's winding trails that stretched for many miles. She thought it was the perfect destination for her peace-finding journey.

JOSHUA TREE NATIONAL PARK

Joshua Tree National Park is a place where two desert ecosystems meet. The Colorado Desert is in the low-elevation eastern side of the park. On the western side, the higher-elevation Mojave Desert stretches as far as the eye can see. The park spans 1,238 square miles (3,208 sq km). It is the second-largest national park in California, with Death Valley being the largest. Joshua Tree National Park has more than 750 plant species, including the Joshua tree. These spiky succulents are actually yucca plants that can live for 150 years.[1]

A ROOKIE MISTAKE

That morning before she left for the hike, Nelson packed her bag full of snacks, including a protein bar and a bagel. She also brought a straw hat, sunscreen, and

▲ Joshua trees can reach 20 to 40 feet (6–12 m) tall. They have spiky leaves at the ends of their branches.

▲ Lost Palms Oasis is in Lost Palms Canyon. The only palm native to the area, the California fan palm, grows here.

plenty of water to make sure she didn't get dehydrated in the desert heat. Then she drove to the Joshua Tree visitor center to pick up a park map and find out more about the trail system.

Nelson looked for a moderate walk to try. Though she was an experienced hiker, she didn't want to take on too much this early in her stay. She would tackle the harder hikes later in the week after she had built up her stamina. She decided on the Lost Palms Oasis Trail, which was 7.5 miles (12 km) out and back.[2] She was sure she could easily tackle that in a day and be home in time for dinner.

Nelson's hike should have been a breeze. But she made a mistake before setting out on the trail at 9:15 a.m. She texted

Lou the night before about her plans to hike the trail and asked a park ranger for directions to the trailhead that morning. But she didn't tell any family or other close friends about her plans for the day. If anything out of the ordinary happened, no one would be able to help her.

CATASTROPHE STRIKES

The first part of the Lost Palms Oasis Trail was stark but beautiful. There was plenty of brush, and shrubs called ocotillos peppered the landscape. Nelson scrambled over boulder piles and dipped down into desert washes, passing a few other hikers along the way. About two hours into her walk, she noticed something a little strange. The moderate-rated trail seemed harder and more confusing than it should have been. With a sinking feeling, Nelson suddenly understood that she was lost.

TRAIL-RATING SYSTEMS

There is no universal trail-rating system, even for national parks. But many websites or hiking apps will divide hikes into five categories depending on the trail's length and elevation gain: easy, moderate, moderately strenuous, strenuous, and very strenuous. Easy hikes are usually less than three miles (4.8 km) and suitable for most people who enjoy walking. In contrast, very strenuous hikes can extend for more than eight miles (13 km).[3] They may include steep hills, rock scrambling, and stream crossings. Only experienced hikers should tackle these trails.

"I didn't realize it at the time, but I had gone a mile off the trail," Nelson later said. "There are markers that tell you the one-mile [1.6 km] point and the two-mile [3.2 km] point, and I was still looking for the three-mile point."[4]

Nelson climbed up to a peak to see if she could get her bearings. She sat on a boulder and took a few sips of water. Then the unthinkable happened. When she got up to take a look around, she slipped.

"I was testing my footing on some of the rocks and, of course, the rock I chose to put a little bit of weight on slipped straight out from under me," Nelson recalled.[5] As her foot started sliding down the embankment, she tried to grab anything along the way to prevent her from falling farther.

Nelson careened more than 25 feet (7.6 m) down into a canyon.[6] When she hit the ground, she heard a chilling sound. "I heard the crack. I felt it through my entire body and screamed. It was a horrifying moment," she said. "You realize everything you planned has completely changed."[7]

Immediately, Nelson reached for her cell phone,

> **Everything went in slow motion, and I remember my brain telling me you're about to get hurt.**[8]
>
> —Claire Nelson in her book, *Things I Learned from Falling,* 2021

▲ Although high ground can help hikers find their bearings, large rocks and boulders may be unstable. This can make climbing them dangerous.

hoping it hadn't broken in the fall and that she could call 911. Luckily, the phone's screen hadn't shattered. But something else stopped her from getting through to emergency dispatch—the lack of cell signal. "And that's when I started to panic . . . because no one really knows that I'm here and there's no one around. It was really terrifying," Nelson said. "I just started screaming for help and could hear the echoing, but there was nobody around."[9]

Nelson tried to move. She could twist her head, wave her arms around, and wiggle her toes, so she knew she wasn't paralyzed. But she couldn't sit up without excruciating pain shooting up her spine. "I would hear this pop, pop, pop and my pelvis kind of cracked and I would . . . scream in pain," she said.[10]

Now panicked, Nelson yelled again as loud as she could, hoping that someone would hear her. "In my mind, I was going, 'If I scream loud enough, maybe it'll just catch on a breeze and somebody on another part of the park will just happen to hear it.'"[11] But by the time it started to get dark out and the temperature dropped, no one had come to her rescue.

What started out as a leisurely stroll to get some peace of mind had turned into a nightmare. Nelson was desperately alone. She didn't have a tent to sleep in or more clothes to protect herself against the chill. She had a little food and water left, but it wouldn't last long. Worst of all, she had gone off the trail, so even if another hiker did come along the next day, they wouldn't pass her. As Nelson watched the sun set in the sky, a startling thought entered her mind: if she didn't get help soon, she might die in the desert.

SURVIVING IN A HARSH ENVIRONMENT

From the Sahara in Africa to Joshua Tree National Park in California, desert biomes are some of the most awe-inspiring places on Earth. In fact, they are some of the last remaining regions of pure wilderness in the world. Scientists are so intrigued by deserts and the creatures that live there that they even study areas such as the Atacama Desert in Chile for clues about what life might be like on Mars.

But despite their majesty, deserts are also some of the harshest environments on the planet. In the severe desert landscape, getting stranded without any help can be especially traumatizing. With temperatures potentially soaring into triple digits during the day and dropping below freezing at night, survival is challenging—especially without water or supplies.

▼ Deserts are beautiful places, but visitors must come prepared and take precautions to stay safe in these extreme environments.

But people have done so and lived to tell the tale. In 1994, a 39-year-old police officer and former Olympic pentathlete named Mauro Prosperi took part in the Marathon des Sables in the Sahara and got trapped in a sandstorm. He spent nine days wandering alone in the desert before finding his way back to civilization.

In December 2006, Danelle Ballengee took her dog, Taz, out for a trail run in Moab, Utah. Ballengee was a two-time world champion in adventure racing and a seven-time Ironman Triathlon finisher. But when she fell 60 feet (18 m) into a canyon and couldn't move for days, it was up to her dog to save her.[12]

Sixty-two-year-old Donna Cooper and her two teenage passengers nearly died while on a desert road trip in 2010. They got lost in Death Valley, California, and didn't have cell service when their car ran out

A FATAL FALL

Claire Nelson sustained a horrific injury and went through a terrifying ordeal. But some people are even less fortunate. On January 7, 2023, Joshua Tree rangers received a report about an injured hiker who had fallen into Rattlesnake Canyon in the remote Indian Cove area of the park. The San Bernardino County Sheriff's Department Aviation Unit, San Bernardino County Fire Department, and the Morongo Basin Ambulance all raced to the scene. The search and rescue teams did what they could to revive her. But 58-year-old Anna Nuno died from her injuries.

of gas. The women spent days without enough food or water.

In 2019, three people got stranded in the Australian outback when their vehicle became stuck in a dry riverbed. They searched for water and shelter from the sun.

According to David Alloway, desert survival expert and author of the book *Desert Survival Skills*, getting trapped alone in a desert without the proper supplies is a frightening scenario. But the most important thing a person can do in that situation is to remain calm, even if it's scary.

"The biggest killer in any emergency situation is panic. Panic blinds a person to reason and can cause them to compound the emergency with fatal results," Alloway says. "The brain is by far the best survival tool we have. Survival is much more a mental than a physical exercise, and keeping control of the brain is necessary."[13] This mental strength and clarity is one of many factors that have contributed to some of the most incredible stories of desert survival in the world.

> "Deserts are defined by their lack of water. Learn to ration sweat, not water. By staying in the shade, limiting activity to cooler times such as night and using your available water, your chances for survival increase greatly."[14]
>
> —David Alloway, author of *Desert Survival Skills*, 2000

CHAPTER 2

THE DANGERS OF
THE DESERT

Deserts are often thought of as vast areas of land full of rolling, sandy hills with little plant or animal life. While that might be true for some deserts, it is not true for others. In fact, deserts can range in shape and size. They can also have different plants and animals depending on where they are located on the globe.

A desert is defined as an arid place, which means it is very dry. Humidity—water vapor in the air—is also near zero in these extreme climates. Sometimes the little rain deserts get evaporates in the dry air before it reaches the ground. Most deserts receive less than ten inches (25 cm) of precipitation per year, although some in chillier climates may receive more in

◀ Sand dunes, such as those in the Sahara, form when wind blows sand into constantly changing peaks and valleys.

the form of snow.[1] So desert animals usually get the water they need from what they eat.

Some deserts, such as the Sahara, are very hot. There, daytime temperatures can hit 130 degrees Fahrenheit (54°C).[2] Other deserts, such as those in Antarctica or Greenland, are cold. They have short, mild summers and long, cold winters. There, the mean winter daytime temperature can fall between 28 and 39 degrees Fahrenheit (−2–4°C). The mean summer temperature in these cold deserts can be anywhere from 70 to 79 degrees Fahrenheit (21–26°C).[3]

Deserts are found on all seven continents. They cover about one-fifth of Earth's land area and are home to about one-sixth of the world's population. That's about one billion people.[4]

MAJOR DESERT TYPES

Some experts divide deserts into four major types: subtropical, semiarid, coastal, and cold. Different plants and animals live in each type. Subtropical deserts are very hot and dry year-round. Most are located either near the Tropic of Cancer, which is between a latitude of 15° and 30° north of the equator, or along the Tropic of Capricorn, which is between 15° and 30° south of the equator.

North America has four major subtropical deserts.[5] They are the Chihuahuan Desert in the southwestern United States, which runs down into the Central Mexican Highlands; the Sonoran Desert, which covers the northwestern Mexican states and part of the southwestern United States; the Mojave Desert, located mostly in southeastern California and southern Nevada; and the Great Basin, in parts of Nevada, Utah, and eastern California.

Many species thrive in subtropical deserts despite the heat. Ground-hugging shrubs and short trees, such as the California juniper shrub and the mesquite tree, abound. Plants have tiny openings called stomata in their leaves that allow for gas exchange. Some plants keep their stomata closed during the day and open them only at night when the least amount of moisture will evaporate. These plants include yuccas, ocotillos, prickly pears,

TOP FIVE LARGEST DESERTS

Deserts are found on every continent in the world. The five largest deserts are, in order of size, the Antarctic desert, the Arctic desert, the Sahara, the Arabian Desert, and the Gobi Desert. The subtropical Arabian Desert stretches across nine countries.[6] It is the largest desert in Asia and the fourth-largest in the world. The Antarctic desert is the world's largest desert. Ninety-eight percent of it is covered in ice.[7]

▲ This map shows where desert areas are located, excluding the Arctic and Antarctic deserts. Semidesert areas are places that have many of the same characteristics of a desert but receive a little more precipitation.

agaves, and brittlebush. Nocturnal herbivores such as mule deer munch on whatever plants they can find to survive. Rattlesnakes and insects such as tarantula hawk wasps dominate the ground, while cactus wrens, ravens, and red-tailed hawks fly through the sky.

Semiarid deserts aren't as hot as subtropical deserts. They get about 1.5 inches (3.8 cm) of rain per year.[8] Sweeping mountain ranges border the edges of some of these semiarid regions. They block moisture-heavy clouds from reaching the sandy soil. Still, many plants do well in this kind of environment, including the creosote bush, bur sage, whitethorn, catclaw, and jujube. Some have large, spiny stalks, which shield the plants' roots from the sun's harsh rays.

Animals that live in semiarid deserts emerge at night to help them stay cool. Jackrabbits and skunks are common throughout the area. Lizards skitter and snakes slither along the rocky ground, feeding on grasshoppers and ants. Burrowing owls hunt scurrying kangaroo rats that try to hide in underground homes.

Coastal deserts such as the Namib, which runs from Angola to South Africa, and the Atacama Desert in Chile sit along large bodies of water, such as oceans or lakes. Here, the temperatures are moderate, hovering between 55 and 75 degrees Fahrenheit (13–24°C).[9] Nights can be freezing, and foggy days are common. Because of the proximity to water, the soil in coastal deserts is better able to support plant life. Saltbushes, buckwheat, ricegrass, little leaf horsebrush, and black sage cover the rocky ground. Coyotes, badgers, and mountain lions stalk their prey at night. Great horned owls, golden eagles, and bald eagles soar through the air.

Cold deserts, located in Antarctica and in the Arctic, are the largest deserts in the world at 5.5 million and 5.4 million square miles (14.2 million and

▲ Because of the lack of plants in Antarctica, many animals rely on the sea for food.

14 million sq km), respectively.[10] Temperatures hover around freezing or below year-round, and these polar regions get six to ten inches (15–25 cm) of rain annually.[11] Instead of sand, cold deserts are covered in snow, ice, and glaciers. Because of the harsh conditions, few plants can survive there aside from shad scale and sagebrush. Rock ptarmigans perch on rocks and ice floes. Emperor penguins, polar bears, Arctic foxes, and snow leopards hunt for food in subzero temperatures.

CLIMATE DANGERS

Plants and animals have adapted to their desert habitats and do what they can to survive day to day. But for people, living or even spending a short amount of time in any one of these types of deserts can be hazardous. Many problems occur because of the extreme heat or cold, lack of protection from the sun, and little to no access to water. Hypothermia and dehydration are two of the most lethal risks.

Hypothermia happens when the body loses heat faster than it can produce it. This causes the body's temperature to drop below 95 degrees Fahrenheit (35°C).[12] Symptoms include shivering, shallow breathing, a weak pulse, lack of coordination, dizziness, memory loss, and loss of consciousness. When a person develops hypothermia, the heart, nervous system, and other organs don't work properly. Serious cases can lead to heart or respiratory failure and even death.

Dehydration occurs when the body loses more fluid than it takes in, preventing it from functioning properly. It can be caused by not drinking enough water or by other conditions such as a fever, excessive sweating, increased urination, diarrhea, or vomiting. Symptoms include a dry mouth and tongue, sunken cheeks, extreme thirst, dark-colored urine, dizziness, and confusion. If left

> "You can't live without water, and in a desert environment, you can't count on finding it. Arroyos—seasonal streams that run in heavy rain or wet conditions—are bone-dry most of the year, and even normally reliable sources can run out.[13]"
>
> —Adam Roy, Backpacker magazine reporter, 2017

untreated, dehydration can cause urinary tract infections or kidney problems and seizures. In severe cases, the body can go into hypovolemic shock, a condition that happens when low blood volume causes a drop in blood pressure and a decreased level of oxygen in the body.

Extreme heat and prolonged exposure to the sun in a desert climate can cause mild to severe sunburn. It can also cause heatstroke, a serious condition that occurs when the body overheats and its temperature reaches 104 degrees Fahrenheit (40°C) or higher.[14] Symptoms include mental confusion, nausea and vomiting, flushed skin, rapid breathing, a headache, and a racing heart rate. Heatstroke requires emergency medical care as soon as possible. If left untreated, it can lead to brain, heart, or kidney damage, or even death.

Weather in the desert can be erratic. Sandstorms can happen suddenly. Massive swirls

> "When . . . our body gets too hot, things don't work normally. . . . People who have existing heart problems, lung problems, kidney problems, even mental health issues—they get sicker. And even for people who are in generally good health, the heat can be really dangerous if we don't pay attention."[15]
>
> —Dr. Aaron Bernstein, NPR, 2022

⚠️ Dehydration can happen in any climate, but it happens faster in hot climates because the body loses more water through sweat.

of debris envelop everything in their path, last for hours, and completely alter the environment. In some areas, such as Arizona, lightning storms and flash floods can occur if the atmospheric conditions are right. A lightning bolt that strikes a human can kill that person instantly. Grand Canyon National Park has 25,000 lightning strikes per year.[16]

Because the desert climate is usually so dry, a burst of precipitation can cause flooding that sweeps away anything in its path, including trees, animals, people, and cars. "Monsoon storms of considerable violence bring isolated but seemingly impenetrable curtains of precipitation while lightning explodes overhead," writes Susan Strom.

She is a weather photographer nicknamed Lightning Lady who chases storms for a living. Trees can catch fire from lightning sparks, power lines can become uprooted from the force of the rushing water, and mudslides can destroy entire neighborhoods. "Seasoned storm chasers, including myself, will not cross flash floods no matter how tempting," Strom adds.[17]

ENVIRONMENTAL HAZARDS

In addition to being aware of climate dangers, people who live or spend time in the desert must pay attention to their surroundings. Many venomous creatures live in caves or under rocks in the desert, including rattlesnakes, spiders, scorpions, centipedes, and Gila monsters. Being stung or bitten by one of these critters can cause severe disease or death. For example, many types of scorpions live in the Arizona desert. Two of these types contain

WHY SNAKEBITES ARE DANGEROUS

Some snakes are harmless to humans. But some, like the diamondback rattlesnake, can be very dangerous. A venomous snakebite can cause nausea, vomiting, numbness, and blurry vision. Some snakebites are even lethal. Experts say the best thing to do after a snakebite is to remain calm. Panic can lead to an increased heart rate, which spreads the venom faster. Mayo Clinic emergency physician Steven Maher says that people should keep the bitten body part still. They should seek treatment quickly.

enough venom in stingers on their tails to kill a human. Symptoms of a bite or sting include numbness at the sting site, difficulty breathing, and a rapid heart rate.

Getting lost in the desert without sufficient supplies is also relatively common and can be deadly. Visitors who use GPS to get directions may unknowingly follow roads that have long been closed or lead to nowhere. Once lost, people may go looking for a source of water.

Visitors may be fooled by mirages, which are optical phenomena that create the illusion of water. They may come across an oasis, which is a lush, fertile area surrounded by arid desert. An oasis can have a source of water. But a visitor may find the water has temporarily dried up in the summer heat. Whatever the case may be, preparing for health and environmental risks before a trip to the desert is vital to surviving the dangers of these harsh landscapes.

ARE OASES REAL?

Most desert climates are hot and dry with little to no protection from the blazing sun. But there are some areas of vegetation called oases that provide not only shade but also an ample supply of water in the form of a river or small lake. Havasu Canyon, part of the Grand Canyon, is an oasis in the Mojave Desert. Havasu Falls flows from the top of a ledge into the canyon below. The Sahara has a few oases that have become important stops along trade routes. For example, Tafilalt is the largest Saharan oasis in Morocco. It runs along the banks of the Ziz River and is known for its date trees.

CHAPTER 3

CLAIRE IS FOUND

As the sun rose on the morning of May 23, the day after her fateful fall in Joshua Tree National Park, Claire Nelson felt anxious and awful. She had barely slept the night before because of her aching body. The chilly temperatures and lack of sufficient clothing didn't help either. Plus, she couldn't stop her mind from obsessing about all the creatures that might be lurking in the night, ready to pounce as she lay helpless on the ground.

Another dire problem Nelson faced was that by afternoon, her food and water had run out. She had eaten what little remained in her pack, so she tried nibbling on her lip balm for sustenance.

◀ In May, temperatures in Joshua Tree National Park can drop to approximately 50 degrees Fahrenheit (10°C).

MISSING FOR SIX DAYS

Similar to Claire Nelson, 64-year-old Ed Rosenthal was an experienced hiker and loved going on walks by himself in the wilderness. But in 2010, a solo hike in Joshua Tree National Park nearly killed him. Like Nelson, he lost the trail he was on and made a wrong turn. He ended up in a deep canyon. Though he had brought along supplies, including a space blanket, some flares, and a whistle, he soon ran out of food and water. When he was finally found and rescued on the sixth day, he had lost 20 pounds (9 kg) and nearly died from dehydration.[2]

Nothing helped. Eventually she stopped thinking about food altogether. "Hunger felt like an entirely fictional concept to me now," Nelson later said. "My body had shut off my appetite like an electrician turning off the main power, cravings and fancies shut down, . . . everything faded to black."[1]

But the issue Nelson couldn't ignore no matter how hard she tried was her terrible, inescapable thirst. It made her feel lightheaded and weak. The situation had gotten so bad that all Nelson could think about was gulping down her favorite drink, Diet Coke.

"Dehydration is [an awful] business. It starts in the mouth, the initial pang of craving quite subtle and easy to ignore, but the signals get more insistent. Over time your tongue becomes increasingly dry and scratchy, thickening like a woolen mitten, sticking against the sides of your mouth, like Velcro," she later wrote in her journal about her experience. "From there you feel it in your head; a slowly increasing pressure throbs inside your skull, as if your brain is shrinking in on itself, withering like a piece of dried fruit."[3]

By the time night fell, Nelson was parched, cranky, and cold. She fixated on all the time she had wasted back in London, not doing what she really wanted or not expressing how she really felt. If she was going to stay alive, make it past age 36, and improve her life, she knew she'd have to come up with a plan to survive.

PLAN OF ACTION

For the next two days, Nelson tried to be proactive despite her inability to move too far from the spot where she had fallen. During the day, she used the supplies in her daypack—a park map, a bandana, and a spare T-shirt—to cover her body to prevent a bad sunburn. She also made a makeshift umbrella out of a grocery bag, her straw hat, and her hiking stick.

> "I was wasting so much of my life on the internet, on social media, using it as a way to just really curate the best parts of myself and keep the parts of myself I was ashamed of hidden away.[4]
>
> —Claire Nelson, 2021

▲ As in many deserts, there is little natural shade in Joshua Tree National Park. Joshua trees' narrow branches do little to block the sunlight, and most other desert plants are short.

To keep herself clean, Nelson used tweezers to cut off her underwear so she could urinate without getting herself dirty. She peed into an empty water bottle and started

drinking the urine because she thought it would help her stay hydrated. She said, "I figured this is something you do when you run out of water because what else is there?"[5]

> **DRINKING URINE**
>
> When stuck in a survival situation, many people sip their own urine in order to stay hydrated. But experts say this move isn't beneficial or healthy and might even make the situation worse. Urine contains high levels of sodium, which gets more concentrated the more dehydrated a person gets. Excess salt can lead to increased thirst. Urine also contains harmful bacteria and toxins from the body. Ingesting these toxins again can cause infection or damage kidney function.

Finally, Nelson did her best to stay calm. When she wasn't yelling to see if anyone could hear her, she took pictures of her surroundings. She also recorded videos on her phone for her loved ones just in case she made it out of the desert alive—or in the worst-case scenario, if she didn't. She said, "I would think of the people in my life I wanted to see again. I was thinking of goals I still had for myself. And I am a very stubborn person. . . . Those things can really keep you going when everything else is against you."[6]

RUMBLING IN THE SKY

By the fourth day alone in the desert, Nelson could barely keep her eyes open and was drifting in and out of consciousness. But little did she know, a rescue mission was underway. Nelson's friend Natalie noticed that Nelson hadn't posted on social media in a while or answered her texts.

▲ The Riverside County Sheriff's Department has multiple helicopters to help with patrols as well as search and rescue.

Natalie started calling around to see if anyone knew where Nelson was.

On May 25, a mutual friend stopped by the house Nelson was watching and found a schedule of all the things that Nelson planned to do in the area. Under May 22, Nelson had listed the Lost Palms Oasis hike. The friend reported her missing to Joshua Tree authorities. Not long after, Nelson's car was spotted in the trailhead parking lot.

A ground and air search immediately got underway. Just a few hours later, a Riverside County Sheriff's Department helicopter team spotted Nelson from above. Nelson heard the rumbling from below. She screamed as loud as she could and waved her makeshift umbrella in the air.

The helicopter circled back and forth overhead. Finally, Nelson heard the words that she had dreamed about but thought she would never live to hear. "Claire! We see you," a voice yelled from the helicopter. "We're going to come and get you!"[7]

Nelson sobbed with joy. Because there was no safe place for the helicopter to land, a rescue crew hiked in to get her. Then the ground rescue crew moved Nelson onto a stretcher, which was hoisted into the air by a crane so she could be loaded into the helicopter. From there, she was transferred to an air ambulance at Chiriaco Summit and flown to Desert Regional Medical Center, where she received treatment for her injuries.

TYPES OF SEARCH AND RESCUE

When people get stranded in the wilderness and can't make it out on their own, a search and rescue team is needed. There are five major types. Ground (lowland) rescue involves looking for people who are lost on mostly level land. Mountain rescues try to extract injured people on rugged terrain or in caves and take them to safety. Urban rescues help people trapped in collapsed buildings in cities. Combat rescue teams look for soldiers and civilians who are injured during a war. Maritime and air-and-sea search and rescue missions try to save sailors and passengers who are lost at sea or survived a crashed aircraft or sinking boat.

AN EMOTIONAL RETURN

Nelson's recovery took nearly a year. But by the time she was feeling better, the once-stranded hiker knew she would have to go back to the scene of her near-certain demise in order to move on with her life. In January 2019, she returned to Joshua Tree National Park. With more than a little anxiety, she hiked the Lost Palms Oasis Trail. But this time, she wasn't alone. She retraced her steps with friends. "Something about it, I guess, was about wanting to get closure—to feel like this hadn't got the better of me," she said.[8]

In 2021, Nelson published a memoir about her Joshua Tree experience called *Things I Learned from Falling*. She began to explore trails in other parts of the world too. Her friends and family thought it unwise to take the risk again. But Nelson was determined to make the most of her life after surviving such an ordeal. "Some people said, 'Well, why would you want to go hiking again?' It's because I love it and now I'm not going to die, which means I get to do more of it," she said.[9]

> **Finished the unfinished hike. The hike that almost finished me. Learned from my failures and finally succeeded. Thankful doesn't even begin to cut it.**[10]
>
> —Claire Nelson, 2019

CHAPTER 4

THE RACE TO NOWHERE

The Sahara is the third-largest desert and the largest hot-weather desert in the world.[1] It is about the size of the entire United States. The Sahara is an extreme environment and one of the hottest places on Earth. The surface temperature of its dunes can reach up to 136 degrees Fahrenheit (58°C).[2]

Few plants or animals can survive in the Sahara because of the excessive heat and lack of rainfall. The region has been compared to the polar ice caps or the surface of the moon, but instead of being cold, it is sandy and scorching hot. Every year in southern Morocco, a marathon nicknamed the Toughest Footrace on Earth takes place in the Sahara.

◀ The Marathon des Sables is now a large event, with 140 volunteers and 450 support staff.

Its official name is the Marathon des Sables, or "Marathon of the Sands."

For six days, participants run for more than 155 miles (250 km) across the desert.[3] They climb up and down sand dunes, across salt plains, and through sparse terrain in search of the finish line. They carry everything they might need on their backs, with water given to them at checkpoints along the way.

The event's website describes the Marathon des Sables as "a truly grueling multi-stage adventure in one of the world's most inhospitable environments, the Sahara Desert." Thousands of people have attempted the race and completed their mission.[4] But in 1994, one Italian man tried to win and almost died in the process.

> "Competing in the Marathon des Sables, a seven-day 'self-sufficiency' endurance race held every spring in the Moroccan Sahara, is the equivalent of running six marathons back-to-back in a convection oven.[5]"
>
> —Hampton Sides, Men's Journal reporter, 2017

TEST OF ENDURANCE

As soon as Mauro Prosperi heard about the race, he knew he had to participate. At 39, he was married and had three children. He worked as a police

▲ It's important to seek shelter during a sandstorm. Tents protect runners in the Marathon des Sables from blowing sand.

officer and was a former Olympic pentathlete. He felt up for the task. "I love a challenge so I started training immediately, running 40 km (25 miles) a day, reducing the amount of water I was drinking to get used to dehydration. I was never home," he said.[6]

On April 10, 1994, Prosperi and the other 133 competitors began the race.[7] At first, everything was fine. Prosperi made good time and enjoyed the scenery. But on April 14, disaster struck. On that particular morning, he was ahead of his running partner, Giovanni Manzo, when a sandstorm hit. The wind was so fierce that it blocked Prosperi's vision and clouded everything in sight. He wrapped a scarf around his head to protect his eyes and face. The storm lasted for several hours. By the time it was over, it was dark out, and Prosperi was so exhausted that he decided to sleep.

The next morning, the landscape had been transformed into something unrecognizable. Though Prosperi had supplies—a pocketknife, a map, a compass, a sleeping bag, and plenty of dehydrated food—he had no idea where he was. He was also running out of water. He urinated into a bottle and saved it just in case things got desperate.

That whole afternoon, Prosperi walked and ran for hours at a time, trying to find someone who could help him. He saw no one, and everything around him looked exactly the same. Manzo had already reported him missing when Prosperi hadn't shown up at the water checkpoint. Officials had halted the race and issued a call for a search and rescue mission.

On April 15, race officials got in Land Rovers and a helicopter and began the search. The Moroccan military also joined in. They knew

THE SCIENCE OF SANDSTORMS

Sandstorms can be terrifying events. But they are common in dry or semiarid areas. They are usually caused by thunderstorms, which increase wind speeds over a wide swath of land. When this happens, the sand and dust on the ground get whipped up into the sky. In a sandstorm, the plumes of swirling dust and sand can sometimes be blown hundreds or even thousands of miles away.

they were running out of time because Prosperi had only a little water. Temperatures were supposed to be in the triple digits. If they didn't find him soon, he would die of heatstroke or dehydration. But though they searched far and wide, Prosperi was nowhere to be found.

GIVING UP HOPE

Meanwhile, Prosperi continued to live out his worst nightmare in the desert. As the sun bore down on him, he walked in the sweltering heat. Just when he thought he couldn't go on any longer, he stumbled upon an abandoned Islamic shrine, a type of religious structure found throughout the Sahara. He used the shrine as a shelter from the unrelenting high temperature and dusty air. He scrawled the letters *SOS* in the sand in case any helicopters overhead could see them.

▲ Today helicopters monitor the progress of the racers throughout the race.

By this point, Prosperi had run out of food and was so thirsty he could barely stand. He sucked on rocks and ate lizards. He also found a colony of bats roosting in the

eaves of the shrine. Desperate for any kind of nutrients, he strangled some of them and gnawed on their flesh. He also sucked their blood. "It was a repellent thing to do, but I was crazed with hunger," he said. "All I tasted was something warm and salty in my mouth."[8] He later found a puddle and was able to rehydrate a little.

After nearly three days of searching and finding nothing, Prosperi's rescue team had given up hope of spotting him. On Saturday, April 16, race officials stopped the search effort so the other runners could keep going. "We hated to leave, because all we could think about was Prosperi out there alone, dying," said British runner René Nevola, who had met Prosperi earlier in the race. "Everyone's morale was incredibly low."[9]

On Sunday, April 17, the first runners crossed the finish line. A banquet was held to celebrate the participants. But the mood in the room was somber. Some of the other runners were already referring to Prosperi in the past tense. "The spirit of the race was ruined," race director Patrick Bauer said. "There was nothing to celebrate."[10] It seemed as though everyone had accepted that Prosperi was dead.

A MIRACULOUS RECOVERY

Unlike the race officials, Prosperi's brother-in-law and brother had not given up on finding him alive. They organized their own rescue party. On April 20, six-and-a-half

▲ With no shade in parts of the Sahara, runners face many potential health risks, including heatstroke and sunburn.

days into Prosperi's ordeal, they found a water bottle and an emergency blanket that belonged to Prosperi near the Morocco-Algeria border. A few days later, they stumbled upon one of Prosperi's shoelaces.

What they didn't know then was that Prosperi had left the shrine a few days before and had started walking, thinking he could find civilization. He did his best to survive. He walked at dawn and dusk. He slept buried in the sand at night for warmth. He occasionally dropped items such as a sock or toothpaste so rescuers might find them.

On the ninth day Prosperi stumbled upon what appeared to be a caravan of Tuaregs, nomadic people who live near the Sahara. After seeing a bedraggled stranger with a disoriented look dressed in racing clothing, they carried Prosperi on a camel to the nearest village and turned him over to the military. The military took him to a doctor. When Prosperi's wife got the call from the authorities that her husband was found alive, she fell to the floor in shock and relief.

It turned out that in all his wandering, Prosperi had walked over the Jbel Bani, a mountain range in the Sahara. Then he crossed the border between Morocco and Algeria, an area thought to be covered in land mines. Overall, he had traveled approximately 130 miles (210 km) from the area where he'd disappeared.[11]

By the time Prosperi arrived at the hospital, he had

THE TUAREG

The Tuareg are a seminomadic group of people who live throughout the Sahara. They inhabit a large area including Mauritania, Algeria, Burkina Faso, Niger, and Libya. The Tuareg are sometimes called Blue People because of the color of their clothing. They are descendants of the Berber, or Amazigh, people of North Africa.

lost approximately 33 pounds (15 kg). That was about 20 percent of his body weight. He sobbed when he heard his wife's voice over the phone: "My skin is like that of a tortoise," he told her from the hospital. "Don't worry, Cinzia. I'm still beautiful."[12]

In the days and weeks that followed, Prosperi became both an honored celebrity and a person of mystery. Though most people took his story at face value, others, including some journalists, insisted Prosperi and his wife had made up the whole story as a publicity stunt to attract fame.

But Prosperi insisted his gaunt physical appearance and poor health told the true story. "They said we planned the whole thing so we could make a pile of money," his wife, Cinzia Pagliara, told a *Men's Journal* reporter. "If that was the case, then you've never met two people who are more stupid than we are."[13]

> "Mauro didn't lie. . . . [His] body provides compelling testimony to the kind of damage the desert can inflict and, at the same time, evidence of what the body can sustain when pushed to its extremes. He competed against the desert as a decided underdog, but he won, turning in the performance of his life.[14]"
>
> —Dr. Kenneth Kamler in his book *Surviving the Extremes,* 2004

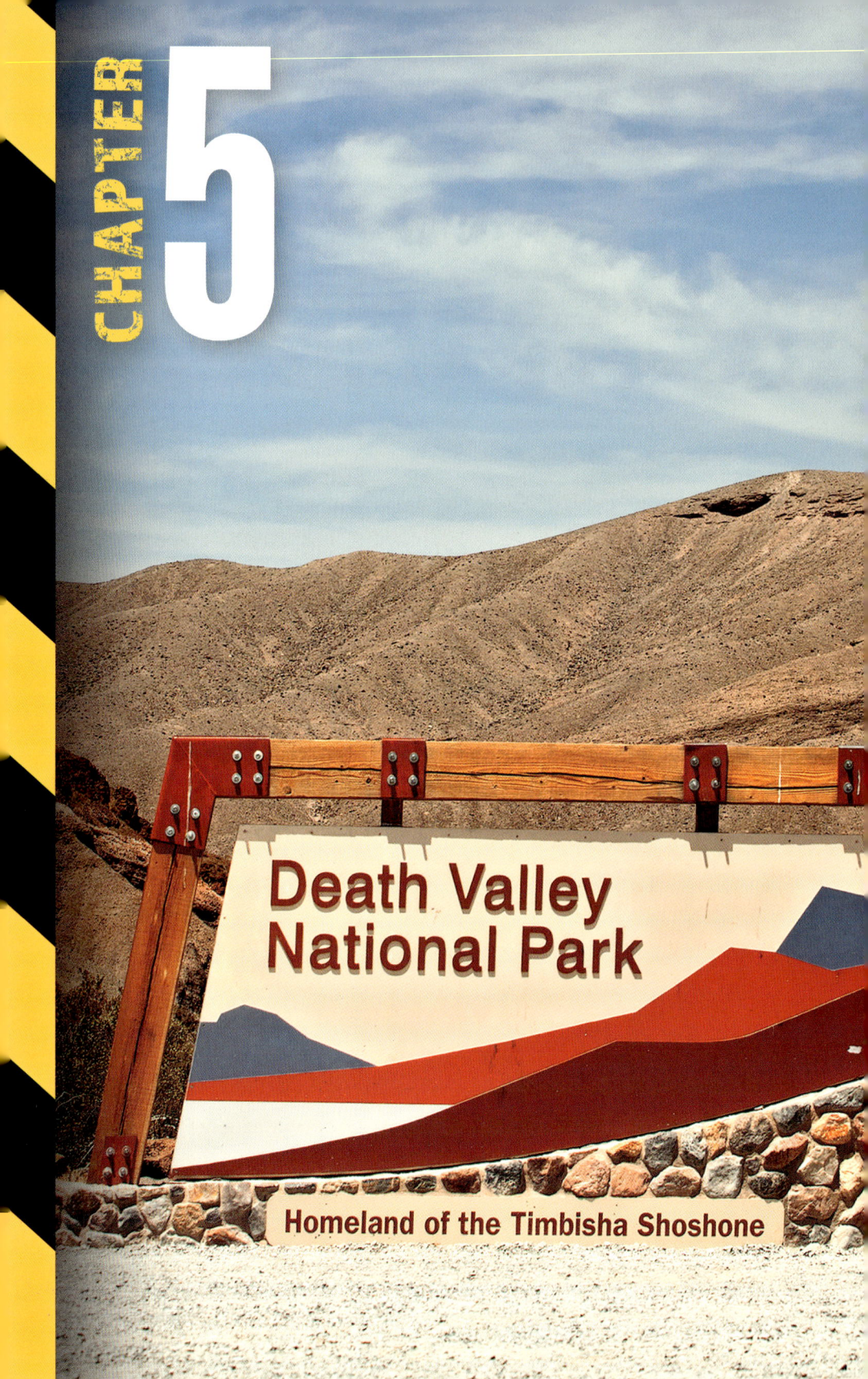

CHAPTER 5

A ROAD TRIP
GONE WRONG

In July 2010, 62-year-old Donna Cooper needed a break from her routine. She wanted to do something she'd never done before. She got in her car with her 17-year-old daughter, Gina, and her 19-year-old houseguest, Jenny Leung, and started driving.

The Coopers lived in Pahrump, Nevada, a town about 60 miles (97 km) from an entrance to Death Valley National Park in California.[1] This national park stretches for more than 5,300 square miles (13,700 sq km) along California's southeastern border. It's full of large sand dunes and arid, scrubby mountains. With temperatures often reaching higher

◀ Death Valley is part of the Timbisha Shoshone's ancestral homeland. They continue to live in Death Valley and the surrounding area and have a reservation within the national park.

than 100 degrees Fahrenheit (38°C) and annual rainfall totaling just 2.2 inches (5.6 cm), it's the hottest, driest place in North America.[2] It's also an easy place to lose one's bearings.

Cooper had been to Death Valley many times before, but there were still some areas she'd never seen. On that scorching July day, she decided it was time to check out an attraction called Scotty's Castle, a sprawling Spanish-style mansion built deep in the desert in the 1920s.

Though the day of exploration started out as fun, the adventure soon turned into a disaster. After Scotty's Castle, the women tried to make their way to another Death Valley attraction called Racetrack—a dry, cracked lake bed where large boulders seem to have moved on their own in straight lines across the ground. The trio never got there because Cooper

SCOTTY'S CASTLE

Scotty's Castle is a huge, sprawling mansion in the northern part of Death Valley National Park. It was constructed in the 1920s as a vacation home for banker Albert Mussey Johnson and his wife, Bessie. They shared the house with their friend, gold prospector Walter Scott. Today the National Park Service owns the mansion. Visitors can take a ticketed underground mystery tour to walk through the tunnels that run under the building. They can also view much of the original furniture, lavish decorations, ornate artwork, and clothing owned by the Johnsons.

▲ Scotty's Castle closed in 2015 after a flood damaged it. The National Park Service began working to restore the building.

took a wrong turn. She tried to retrace her route, but soon they were in an unfamiliar area. To make matters worse, the temperature outside the car had reached a dangerous 125 degrees Fahrenheit (52°C). "I want to go home," Gina told her mother.[3]

RUNNING OUT OF SUPPLIES

Before getting too far off track, Cooper tried using the GPS for directions. But GPS devices don't always work properly in remote or rural areas. Sometimes the database's maps are out of date. Other times, smaller roads that appear in real life don't register on the GPS. According to Death Valley park ranger Charlie Callagan, people who follow the GPS in Death Valley will almost certainly lose their way and not get where

CULTURAL IMPACT
UNRELIABLE GPS

Donna Cooper and the girls could have died in the desert after following poor GPS directions and getting lost. But Death Valley National Park ranger Charlie Callagan says Cooper is not the only person who has made the mistake over the years. "It's what I'm beginning to call death by GPS," he said. "People are renting vehicles with GPS and they have no idea how it works and they are willing to trust the GPS to lead them into the middle of nowhere."[4]

The problem got so bad that park officials took the matter into their own hands. They posted heat-danger warning signs at roadside exhibits. They added a notice to the park website about not relying on cell phones or GPS. They also asked technology companies to remove dangerous or closed roads from GPS maps.

Callagan partnered with a GPS company called TomTom to update or remove a number of roads in their Death Valley maps. He did the same for Navteq and Google Earth too. "It's important for people to know that only a tiny portion of Death Valley has cell phone reception," search and rescue coordinator Micah Alley said about the problem. "GPS units are not only fallible but send people across the desert where no road exists."[5]

they need to go. Cooper later described that their GPS kept telling them to turn after a certain distance or take a U-turn, but it never directed them to anywhere in particular.

The Coopers were also running out of supplies. Most importantly, they didn't have enough water. They had brought along four 16-ounce (0.5 L) bottles for the day's excursion, but assuming they'd be home in time for a refill, they had finished most of the water earlier in the afternoon.[6] Cooper had packed extra sweaters and shoes for the girls to account for the change in temperature late in the day. She had also stashed an emergency blanket and a first aid kit in the trunk of the car in case of an accident. But she and the girls were low on food. They had two apples, a bag of chips, and some cookies left in the car. In addition, the car was running out of gas. Cooper had no idea if she was near any of the park's few gas stations.

Without a better idea about what to do, Cooper followed the GPS directions, hoping to find a road that led to the highway. The gas gauge inched toward empty until the car overheated and stopped moving altogether. Since leaving Scotty's Castle,

> **I was like, 'I don't want to die here. Nobody's ever going to find us.'[7]**
>
> —Gina Cooper, 2013

DEATH VALLEY WILDLIFE

Death Valley is full of animals that thrive in the hot desert environment. Coyotes, roadrunners, ravens, ground squirrels, and lizards are the most commonly seen wildlife in the area. Desert bighorn sheep climb up the craggy cliffs and can go days without drinking water. Desert tortoises feed off the wildflowers, grasses, and cacti in Death Valley. They sleep underground. The Devils Hole pupfish is found in the water-filled cavern of the same name that extends below the side of a craggy hill. This fish is one of the rarest in the world. It is the only type of fish that can survive in Devils Hole's hot water, which is 93 degrees Fahrenheit (34°C).[10]

Cooper had driven more than 200 miles (320 km). With no other place to go, the women slept in the car that night. The whole time, the girls tried not to freeze and worried about wild animals attacking the car. "Don't be scared," Cooper said. "We just need a plan."[8]

A CRY FOR HELP

The next morning, Cooper and the girls peeled cacti, hoping to find liquid inside to drink. They also did everything they could think of to attract attention in case someone happened to drive by. They made a big message out of rocks in the sand that said, "HELP, CALL POLICE" and wrote the same words in the dust on the back of their car.[9] They waved the yellow emergency blanket in the air whenever an airplane flew by. They even used an old CD as a signal mirror, hoping the flashy glint would catch a pilot's eye. As a last resort, they tried to build a fire using twigs, brochures from Scotty's Castle, and the car's cigarette lighter, but the kindling wouldn't catch.

When nothing else worked, Cooper tried again to get the car to start. After a few fits and starts, the engine turned over. Cooper drove back toward a locked gate and an abandoned campsite with a few abandoned trailers and other structures the girls had spotted the day before. Though they normally would never break into someone else's property, Cooper figured this was a life-and-death situation. She found a screwdriver and crowbar and pried open one of the doors.

Inside one of the trailers, the women found empty jars, which they filled with water from a hose outside. They also found cans of beans, some spaghetti, and instant ramen, which they ate.

Leung tried to use a radio she discovered in a pile on a table, but it produced

DRINKING CACTUS WATER

A common myth is that drinking liquid from a cactus is a safe bet if a person gets stranded in the desert without water. This isn't true. According to experts, the liquid inside cacti isn't actually water. It is a jellylike fluid that can be harmful to people. Drinking this liquid can cause severe vomiting and diarrhea, which can make the body even more dehydrated. In extreme situations, a fishhook barrel cactus is the only safe cactus to cut open and drink from, but only in small doses.

only static. Cooper was running out of ideas, but at least she and the girls had found shelter from the blazing heat.

HELP FROM FAMILY

Cooper and the girls tried everything they could think of to get themselves to safety. But their rescue was facilitated thanks to Cooper's husband, Rodger, who was visiting one of the Coopers' other daughters, Sky, in Florida. Rodger thought it strange that his wife hadn't called after her road trip to Scotty's Castle, but he wasn't too concerned because she often changed plans.

But Sky, who had just undergone gallbladder surgery the following morning, became concerned when her mother didn't check in to see how it had gone. She checked Cooper's social media accounts and credit card. The last charge Cooper made was at Scotty's Castle. Sky called Charlene Dean, one of Cooper's neighbors, to see if Dean had heard or seen anything, but she had not.

That afternoon, Sky and Rodger called the supermarket where Cooper worked. They were even more surprised to find out that she hadn't reported to work when she was scheduled. Sky and her father knew something must be terribly wrong.

▲ Visitors to Death Valley can drive for miles in some areas without seeing another car.

▲ National park rangers, including those in Death Valley, can have a variety of roles, from education to law enforcement or emergency response.

Sky and Dean called the sheriff's departments in a few different counties, the California Highway Patrol, and the ranger station at Death Valley National Park. A search and rescue team was dispatched throughout the area. By 5:00 p.m. on the third day after getting lost, Cooper and the girls had been located. Leung had gone outside to wave the emergency blanket around in the air, and a California Highway Patrol helicopter spotted her. "I've never been so happy to see anything in my life," Cooper told ABC News.[11]

Upon landing, the emergency medical technicians (EMTs) checked the trio and made sure they weren't hurt. Then they radioed a backcountry campground operator, who drove over with a tank's worth of gas and directions back to the highway. Cooper remains wary of following GPS directions in rural areas after her experience in Death Valley. Whenever possible, she takes a physical map along just in case.

> "If they were not found that day by us or somebody else, they would have perished.[12]
>
> —EMT and California Highway Patrol pilot Tyler Johns, 2013

CHAPTER 6

TAZ TO
THE RESCUE

When Danelle Ballengee woke up on December 13, 2006, she decided it was an ideal day to get outdoors. The sun was out. The sky was a beautiful blue—perfect for an eight-mile (13 km) trail run on the Amasa Back Trail.[1] At the time, 35-year-old Ballengee lived in Dillon, Colorado, a small, mountain-flanked town. Dillon was located near several ski resorts and full of scenic vistas. Ballengee loved hiking and running in the region because of its beautiful scenery and promise of solitude.

Ballengee was a two-time world champion in adventure racing, a seven-time Ironman Triathlon finisher, and six-time US Athlete of the Year in four

◀ Danelle Ballengee adopted Taz in 2003 when he was a puppy.

> "She trains 20 to 30 hours a week by just going out and having fun in the mountains. It's amazing, but that's what she does. That's who she is. She's tough as nails."[2]
>
> —Dave Mackey, ultrarunner and adventure racer, about Ballengee, 2011

different sports: adventure racing, duathlon, mountain running, and triathlon. She enjoyed testing her skills and chose varied landscapes full of steep hills to ascend and rocks to scramble over. She felt more alive with every thrill and challenge. Ballengee often brought her dog, Taz, along on whatever trail she was tackling so he could get some exercise and keep her company. He enjoyed running with her for even a couple of hours at a time.

This time, Ballengee and Taz were headed to Moab, a small city in eastern Utah that is known as the gateway to Arches National Park. There the dirt is a rustic red, and the land is peppered with large natural rock formations and scrub trees. Ballengee got a kick out of watching Taz sniff under shrubs and chase critters such as snakes and small lizards. Little did she know that her furry companion would be the reason she is still alive today.

A DEVASTATING INJURY

Ballengee was used to taking breaks in her busy day to spend some quality time in the wilderness. An eight-mile

(13 km) trail run would normally take her 90 minutes, so she could break a little sweat, reap the calming benefits, and then get back to work. But this time, about 45 minutes into her trail run, the unthinkable happened. Ballengee stepped on a streak of black ice, which is ice that appears to be a harmless glaze on hard surfaces but is actually very slippery. She lost her balance and slid over the trail's edge. Then she crashed down a steep, icy rock face, tumbled across a few small ledges, and fell 60 feet (18 m) to the ground below.[3]

At the bottom of the canyon, Ballengee wiggled her toes and limbs. Thankfully, she wasn't paralyzed. However, she felt a shooting pain in her backside. She found out later that she had shattered her pelvic bone. But at that moment as she lay there in pain, Ballengee knew she had to find help soon.

In December, Moab temperatures hover around

MOAB: A PLACE OF BEAUTY

Moab is located in the eastern part of Utah. The town attracts a lot of tourists because it is on the Colorado River, where visitors can kayak, fish, and go whitewater rafting. Moab is also near two national parks. Canyonlands National Park is full of rocky cliffs, where many people go climbing and rappelling. Arches National Park is home to more than 2,000 freestanding natural sandstone arch formations. One of the most popular is the massive Delicate Arch. The opening beneath the arch is 46 feet (14 m) high and 32 feet (9.8 m) wide.[4]

▲ The Amasa Back Trail is near the Colorado River. Many visitors enjoy great views.

40 degrees Fahrenheit (4.4°C) during the day. But at night, they can drop below freezing.[5] If Ballengee stayed in one place without moving, she could develop hypothermia.

It took Ballengee five hours to crawl a quarter of a mile (0.4 km).[6] The whole time she kept screaming as loud as she could, hoping that someone would hear her. The only food she had on her was energy gummies, so she ate those sparingly. To stay hydrated, she used her hand to smash through a small ice puddle and drank the muddy liquid.

When the sun went down, Ballengee tried to do some exercises to get her blood circulating and stay warm. Her hands suffered from frostbite. "I moved my head up and down in a 'crunch' motion. I tapped my feet. I rubbed my hands together. I did this for 14 hours, being careful not to fall asleep and freeze to death," she said.[7]

Taz had made his way to her, and throughout the night and into the next night, he mostly stayed by Ballengee's side, with a few jaunts away from the spot where she fell. "The whole time I was thinking, 'I can't die. I'm not ready to die,'" Ballengee said. "It scared me to even think about it, so I just kept fighting and telling myself I just had to stay awake."[8]

WOMAN'S BEST FRIEND

Before Taz saved Ballengee's life, the pair had a long history of friendship and fun. Ballengee got Taz in 2003 when he was ten weeks old. After that, they spent almost every moment together—running, hiking, and just playing in the yard. By the time Taz was two, he and Ballengee were hiking 15 miles (24 km) at a time. On one of their most strenuous adventures, they hiked to the summit of one of Colorado's fourteeners, which is what climbers call mountains that are more than 14,000 feet (4,267 m) high.[9]

RESCUED AT LAST

By the third day, Ballengee began to lose hope that she would ever be found. She became depressed. Tears came to her eyes when she thought about her parents, her sister, her friends, the cute man she had met about a week before leaving for Moab, and the fact that she might never see any of them again.

She made a list of all the places she hadn't yet traveled in the world and wanted to visit. The feelings were overwhelming. She thought about coffee and campfires and other little things in life, realizing she would never get to enjoy them again.

In addition to feeling sadness, Ballengee was more frightened than she'd ever been in her life. She knew it was time to do something drastic. Still in great pain, she rolled over onto her stomach. Then she tried to drag herself up and over a small ledge. It was too large. She switched routes. For the next three hours, Ballengee scooched and tried to shimmy out of the hole where she lay debilitated.

At this point, Ballengee knew she wouldn't be able to get out of the canyon on her own. She rolled over onto her back again to recover. She screamed for someone to notice she was missing.

▲ Even if someone passes near a canyon that a person is stuck in, they likely won't know anyone is there unless the person is conscious and calling for help.

Then, nearly 56 hours after she and Taz embarked on their run, their fortunes changed. Because the duo didn't come home after their outing, Ballengee's family and friends had become worried. Luckily, Ballengee had left the blinds open, the screen door ajar, and the lights on in her house. She had also told a friend she would call him after she came home from the run, but the call never came.

During Ballengee's absence, her neighbor Dorothy Rossignol had called Moab authorities and the National Park Service to alert them about a missing person. At noon on December 16, the local police found Ballengee's pickup truck still parked in the Amasa Back Trailhead lot. They called in a search and rescue team.

Meanwhile, a local who lived in Moab had also called in to report a sighting of a dog that matched Taz's description running alone toward town. Curt Brewer, chief deputy of the Grand

> ### THE SCIENCE BEHIND LIFESAVING DOGS
>
> There are countless stories in the news about dogs that save humans from catastrophes. Scientists aren't totally sure why dogs risk their own lives to protect their humans, but they think it has to do with empathy. Some dogs might respond to "very subtle signals of our emotional states, potentially those that may even not be obvious or conscious to ourselves," says Annika Huber, a doctoral student at Switzerland's University of Bern Veterinary Public Health Institute.[10]

County Sheriff's Office in Moab, explained that they tried to catch the dog, but he ran away, so they followed him.

Taz led Brewer and the Grand County Search and Rescue crew directly to the spot where Ballengee had fallen. "The dog took our rescue personnel right to her," Brewer said. "I think we would have eventually found her because we were in the right location, but the dog saved us some time. And that was important, because if it had gotten dark, that would have complicated things. And it wound up snowing later that night, too."[11]

When the search and rescue team reached Ballengee, tears were streaming down her face. She was overcome with emotion that someone had finally found her and that she wouldn't die shivering and alone. Deliriously, she begged Brewer and his crew to help her. "I'm so glad to see you," Bego Berhart, another crewmember, said in return.[12]

Berhart and the rest of the crew laid her on a stretcher they had brought with them, covered her in a warm sleeping bag, and strapped her in so she wouldn't fall. Then they loaded her into a helicopter and flew her first to St. Mary's Medical Center in Grand Junction, Colorado. She was then transferred to a bigger hospital in Denver, Colorado. There, Ballengee found out she had lost a lot of blood due to internal bleeding. She had surgery to repair her pelvis, which had broken in four places. After inserting two screws and a titanium plate, the doctors told her she was lucky. If it had been any colder, she would have died from hypothermia. If it had been any warmer, she would have bled to death, because warm temperatures cause the blood to be thinner and circulate better, which would have caused her to lose blood more quickly.

A FULL RECOVERY

For Ballengee, the next few months after her accident in Moab were incredibly difficult. She was in significant pain. But with a lot of physical therapy, she made a full recovery. By the following year, Ballengee and Taz were back to trail running.

In May 2007, Taz received the National Hero Dog Award from the Society for the Prevention of Cruelty to Animals in Los Angeles. "It's pretty amazing, what he did," Ballengee says. "We figured he must have run about 15 miles [24 km] when he led the rescuers to me. He definitely helped save my life."[13]

CULTURAL IMPACT
I SHOULDN'T BE ALIVE

After the perilous fall into a canyon in Moab, Danelle Ballengee's life was never the same. Four years after she nearly died, the Discovery Channel made a documentary about her experience. It was an episode in a hit series called *I Shouldn't Be Alive*. After the episode aired, people from all over the world contacted Ballengee to tell her how much her experience moved them.

"This woman had just seen the show they did," Ballengee said. "She was saying how she watched the show in her garage, still sweaty from her workout, and how seeing it got her life turned back around. It's cool hearing that the story inspired her."[14]

But in the years following the accident, Ballengee wasn't just the star of a television show. She also made changes in her personal life. She married B. C. LaPrade, the man she met a few weeks before the accident. The couple has two boys.

After her fall, Ballengee decided she also wanted to do more to give back to her community. She and LaPrade bought Milt's Stop & Eat, a popular diner in Moab. According to Ballengee, running the restaurant is hard work, but it feels like serving food to her extended family and she enjoys owning it.

▲ Ballengee settled in Moab and looks for ways to participate in the community.

CHAPTER 7

TRAPPED IN THE OUTBACK

The outback is a remote, very sparsely populated area in Australia with wide-open spaces and red dirt. The arid desert stretches through sections of the Northern Territory and the states of South Australia, Queensland, and Western Australia. Mulga trees, eucalyptus trees, spinifex grasses, and desert oak trees are sprinkled throughout the region. Its few creeks and rivers, where red kangaroos come to drink, are lined with river gum trees.

Few roads run through the Australian outback's vast expanse. Travelers can drive for hours without seeing another car. Still, many tourists and locals alike

◀ Mulga trees have needlelike leaves that point upward so they get the cooler morning and evening sun but don't get much direct sunlight when the sun is at its hottest high in the sky.

visit the area to go on day hikes, to drive or motorcycle through, or to camp for a few days in one spot. Most bring plenty of water, stockpiles of food and blankets, and extra gas. They go away for the weekend and come back without an issue.

But on rare occasions, visitors to the outback aren't so lucky. Travelers encounter car trouble, get lost or stranded, or die because they aren't prepared for the harsh desert conditions. On some days, temperatures can reach more than 104 degrees Fahrenheit (40°C). "People perish either because their body ran out of fluid, so dehydration, or their body was too hot for too long, causing multi-organ failure and ultimately death," says Dr. Matt Brearley of Australia's Critical Care and Trauma Response Centre.[1]

STUCK IN A RIVERBED

On November 19, 2019, which is springtime in Australia, three friends—52-year-old Tamra McBeath-Riley; her partner, 46-year-old Claire Hockridge; and their friend, 40-year-old Phu Tran—set out on a drive into the outback of the Northern Territory. They brought along McBeath-Riley's dog, Raya, for company. They packed 1.5 gallons (6 L) of water, a package of cookies, and some beef noodles.[2]

Before they left, they told their family and friends where they were going.

The trip was supposed to be short, lasting just an afternoon. McBeath-Riley and the rest of the group had told friends they would just be driving or camping. In reality, they were retrieving a drug stash they had buried a few days earlier. But then their four-wheel-drive truck got stuck in a dry riverbed. They pushed and pulled the rear of the truck, but it wouldn't budge. They stomped on the gas pedal and revved the engine, but the truck's wheels just kept on spinning in place. There was no cell service in the area, so they couldn't call for help.

The trio stayed by the stranded truck for three days, hoping someone would drive by who could bring them

▼ An empty stream may look dry at the surface, but there can be mud just below that can cause vehicles to get stuck.

to safety. To keep cool during the scorching-hot day, they dug a ditch so they could lie down underneath the truck. At night, they slept inside the vehicle and did their best to remain calm.

By the fourth day, the group still hadn't seen anyone. They were also running out of supplies, and there were no trees around for shade. They decided to look for a better spot that would shelter them from the sun. Before leaving, they wrote a note about their plan and left it in the truck, hoping someone would find it.

AN ARDUOUS TREK

About one mile (1.5 km) from the abandoned truck, McBeath-Riley and the others found a watering hole along the Finke River.[3] They had

▲ Even if people in a desert do find water, it may not be safe to drink because of parasites and other contaminants.

barely any food left, but at least they could drink the water to survive. They used a shirt to filter the water as best they could, and then they boiled it to try to kill bacteria. It was still dirty water, but they drank it to stay alive.

By November 28, nearly a week after they had embarked on the trip, the trio became anxious that no one had noticed they were missing. They still hadn't spotted any search and rescue helicopters and worried they would never be found. After many difficult discussions, the group decided to split up. Certain no one was looking for them, they decided someone had to walk to get help. And they figured it would be safer if two people went.

McBeath-Riley knew Raya wouldn't be able to make the journey, so she stayed behind with the dog at the watering hole. Hockridge and Tran planned to walk to the closest highway, which was 14 miles (23 km) away.[5] They brought

▲ If people who are lost follow a river or fence, it may lead to a road or building where they can get help.

along a compass and a GPS device. They followed the Finke River so they would at least have access to water.

AN ASTONISHING RECOVERY

McBeath-Riley and her dog waited three more days at the watering hole, surviving for a total of 12 days in the wilderness. McBeath-Riley hadn't eaten anything for the last five of them and started feeling weak and sick. But on the twelfth day, her hopes of a rescue were finally realized.

Several days earlier, when McBeath-Riley and the others didn't return home when they were expected, her friends had called the local search and rescue organization. In the meantime, a cattle rancher told police he had spotted strange tire tracks in an area where they wouldn't normally have been. The police then informed the search and rescue team. The air search for the missing group was redirected to the correct spot, and it located McBeath-Riley's vehicle. The note left inside led them to her watering hole.

McBeath-Riley was swiftly airlifted to a hospital. She was treated for sun exposure, stomach upset, and dehydration but was otherwise in good spirits. Raya also survived the ordeal.

For Australian officials, McBeath-Riley's rescue after so long a time was a miracle. But unfortunately, Hockridge and Tran were still missing. In an area full of sandy dunes, pockets of trees, and rocky outcrops, the search effort continued to be uncertain and difficult.

A TRAGIC OUTCOME

While McBeath-Riley was recovering in the hospital, the search and rescue team scoured the area for any clues about where the missing parties might be. On December 3, they made a breakthrough. That morning, local farmer Ted Fogarty spotted unfamiliar boot tracks on his remote property. He found a man hiding in one of his large cement water pipes. The man seemed disoriented, dirty, and exhausted. "I picked him up and asked where he was going, if he wanted to come with me," Fogarty said. "[I] took him back to the station and gave him [food], made him a sandwich, and he drank two cans of Coke."[8]

The emaciated man Fogarty found was Tran. But though Tran was now safe, the crew still didn't know where Hockridge was. Two days earlier, Tran and Hockridge had separated at the fence that surrounded Fogarty's vast property. The strategy was for Tran to follow the fence line until he could locate help. Superintendent Pauline Vicary of the Northern Territory Police said the search and rescue team would now switch their efforts to focus on Hockridge's location before she and Tran separated, and they hoped to find her alive.

But the outcome didn't turn out as everyone had hoped. On December 4, authorities found Hockridge's body in the area where Tran had last seen her. McBeath-Riley and Tran were devastated. The story of the trio's harrowing experience and Hockridge's death was reported around the world. In a news conference, Hockridge's sister Sarah told reporters, "We are all grieving and exhausted from the emotional roller-coaster that we've ridden over the past one and a half weeks." She added, "We're really, really grateful to everyone who's supported us through what has been a tremendously difficult, agonizing time."[9]

> "[Tran] is just so lucky he come into here, like he could have went anywhere, and you wouldn't have got water for another 20 [km (12 miles)]."[10]
>
> —Ted Fogarty, 2020

CHAPTER 8

SURVIVING
THE DESERT

Getting lost or stuck in the desert is a terrifying ordeal. But even people who don't get stuck, lost, or injured while in a desert environment need to take precautions. Whether it's making a home in the desert, driving through it in a car, or hiking through it on foot, experts say people should take several steps to ensure they're fully prepared. "Learning to be part of the desert's ecosystem is the first step of desert survival," says David Alloway, author of *Desert Survival Skills*. "My philosophy is not to fight the desert, but to become part of its ecosystem. Being prepared is an obvious benefit."[1]

◀ Deserts offer sights that can't be found anywhere else. Preparation can help people exploring deserts stay safe and enjoy their trip.

> Take a good drink when you need it. People have been found dead from dehydration with water in their canteens.[3]
>
> —David Alloway, author of *Desert Survival Skills*, 2000

STAY HYDRATED

There aren't many dependable, naturally occurring sources of water in desert climates aside from rare oases, although they too may be dry at times. Therefore, staying hydrated throughout the journey is key to surviving. For hiking on foot, most experts recommend carrying at least one to 1.5 gallons (3.8–5.7 L) of water per person, per day. If in a car, bringing even more per person is best.[2] Hikers, bikers, and runners should take account of how much water is in their supply and turn back toward the trailhead when the amount is half gone.

In addition to water for people, water and enough gas for vehicles is important too. Gas stations and convenience stores are few and far between in some desert climates. Drivers should keep extra supplies such as gas, water specifically for the car, and coolant in the trunk in case the vehicle overheats. Coolant, which contains antifreeze, pulls heat away from the engine. A car or truck engine is more likely to overheat if the coolant supply is low. Keeping the levels topped off is the best way to avoid any emergencies. Water can also help cool off the engine temporarily.

▲ People visiting deserts should make sure they have plenty of water. They also need to have enough water for any children or pets with them.

WEAR THE RIGHT CLOTHING

Most desert climates are blazing hot. For many people, it can be tempting to wear as little clothing as possible to stay cool, especially when doing something active, such as running or backpacking. But this is often a mistake. Layering is the smartest way to stay prepared for when the temperatures are high during the day and cold in the evening.

Lightweight, light-colored, loose-fitting clothing made from natural fibers such as linen, hemp, cotton, or wool is best. Wearing breathable, airy shirts and long pants can decrease the risk of overheating, slow down dehydration, and provide a barrier against the wind. Some clothing has an ultraviolet protection factor (UPF) of 50 built into its fabric, which shields any skin beneath it from the sun's rays.

Sunglasses and a broad-brimmed hat are also a must for sun protection. "Your head is the most important tool you have in any situation, so you need to protect it well," writes Cory Doggett in his outdoor blog, Trek Southwest. "Additionally, the back of your neck and shoulders are some of the most exposed areas of your body when you're outside. If you head out for a desert hike without protective head gear, you're asking for trouble."[4]

Closed-toe shoes with traction, such as hiking boots, are important for keeping feet stable and supported. Hiking boots have higher rims that support the ankles and can prevent sprains on rocky trails. They also protect the ankles from thorns. The soles should be stiff enough to protect

▶ DESERT ADVENTURE CHECKLIST

It's important to have a checklist of items to bring before going on a desert adventure. Everyone's list will be a bit different based on their own needs and where they are visiting.

CLOTHING AND GEAR

 BACKPACK  SUNGLASSES 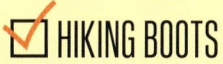 HIKING BOOTS  HAT

TOOLS

 POCKETKNIFE  GPS  MAP

HEALTH AND WELLNESS

   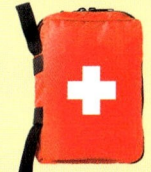

☑ WATER  FOOD  SUNSCREEN  FIRST AID KIT

against rough rocks and not wear out too quickly but soft enough to provide good grip.

BUY THE RIGHT SUNSCREEN

Sunscreen is also very important in the desert, but bringing along the right sunblock isn't as simple as it sounds. Not all sunscreens are the same. Some kinds, such as oils or sunblock with a low sun protection factor (SPF) number, are less effective in protecting the skin from the sun and preventing harmful sunburns that can lead to melanoma, the most serious type of skin cancer. Outdoor guide and REI blogger Annemarie Kruse suggests using water- or sweat-resistant sunblock because the product won't wash off as quickly during active afternoons when shade is hardest to find. "Choose a sunscreen with broad-spectrum protection, this means it blocks UVA and UVB rays," she said. "The SPF level should be 30 or higher. The more intense the sun, the more often you should re-apply."[6]

PACK ENOUGH GEAR

Backpacks can get heavy, but it's important to bring along safety supplies in case of emergencies, especially in the desert. Items such as a police-style whistle, a small mirror, and aluminum foil are great tools to use for signaling and can be seen or heard from miles away. If there's room, a shiny fold-up Mylar blanket found at camping stores can be useful. The blanket can serve as an extra layer to prevent hypothermia and as a signaling device to wave in the air to catch a search and rescue helicopter's attention.

A pocketknife or Swiss Army knife serves many purposes in a desert survival kit. It can be used to cut up food, shred clothing for a tourniquet after an injury, or provide protection in dangerous situations. Compasses are essential for telling direction, and waterproof matches or flint and steel are smart to have on hand in case a fire is needed for warmth or to attract attention. Headlamps or small flashlights help hikers who are stranded in the desert see in the dark.

For minor medical emergencies, a first aid kit is indispensable for dressing small wounds. It should include bandages and pain killers. Antibacterial ointment, antiseptic cream, or alcohol wipes can be used to prevent infection. A triangle bandage and gauze can be used to create a makeshift splint for more serious injuries such as broken arms. Bug spray can provide protection against mosquitoes.

A filter straw, water filter, ultraviolet (UV) light, or water purification tablets to ward off waterborne diseases are a must if there will be any natural water source on the trip that might contain contaminants. Each device has a different level of usage. UV lights kill pathogens in small amounts of mostly clear water, but they don't work well on muddy or sandy water from a stream. Water purification tablets such as Aquatabs are effective against viruses, bacteria, and giardia, but they don't protect against cryptosporidia, microscopic parasites that cause long-lasting diarrhea. Purification tablets also can't filter out debris. Many outdoor experts consider portable reverse-osmosis water filters to be a smart first line of defense. They can filter out muck, parasites, bacteria, and viruses.

Lastly, although for many people the point of taking an excursion in nature is to get away from technology, some

▲ A good hiking backpack can help desert explorers comfortably carry everything they need for themselves as well as for others.

tech gadgets can make any desert trip much safer in the long run. A solar charger uses energy from the sun to charge devices such as cell phones. Hikers often rely on Garmin or other GPS devices for downloadable topographic maps that can be used in tandem with a cell phone but can also be accessed in areas without cell service.

   Though they can be expensive, satellite phones are phones that connect directly with orbiting communication satellites in space instead of relying on cellular service. They require a view of the sky to function, working best on cloudless days. With a satellite phone, a stranded person can send out an SOS signal to a local emergency number, send and receive phone calls, and send short text messages. If all else fails, personal locator beacons (PLBs) can be activated. "A PLB is a small transmitter that sends out a personalized emergency distress signal to the nearest rescue service," says DesertUSA Newsletter journalist Felice Prager. "They are becoming a highly effective and internationally recognized way of summoning help, though they should be used only in life-threatening situations."[8]

ALERT LOVED ONES

One of the most important things a person can do before embarking on a trip into the desert is to tell someone where they're going and when they plan to be back. That way, if something doesn't go as planned, the family member, friend, or coworker can alert a park ranger, a search and rescue team, or the police. Information to give this person includes the route the adventurer will be taking and the vehicle being driven as well as how to get in contact.

It's important to update this person if plans change. Though it might seem like overkill, Prager suggests also

▲ Hiking alone can make rescue less likely if an accident happens. But whether hiking alone or in a group, people should always be prepared.

providing friends and family with the contact information of any travel companions, a list of health issues and medications, and any emergency supplies brought along on the trip.

Additionally, some trailheads have information cards for desert adventurers to fill out. They're usually located in a box by the wall maps of the area. People should be sure to fill in all the details, most importantly the in-and-out dates of their excursion. The information on these cards can help people be found more quickly in an emergency.

WHAT TO DO IN AN EMERGENCY

Millions of people head out into the world's deserts each year. It's possible to spend time in a desert environment and enjoy the experience without trouble. But emergencies do happen. People should camp on high ground, but not on top of exposed peaks or ridges in case of a thunder or lightning storm. They should avoid deep canyons and dry washes, especially during stormy weather. If heavy rains occur, hikers and explorers should move as high up as possible right away—at least 30 to 40 feet (9–12 m) above the canyon floor or bottom of the dry wash—to avoid being swept away in a flash flood.[9]

> "With a bit of knowledge and a lot of common sense, tragedies can be avoided. There is no such thing as being too prepared when you are in an environment that can pose danger. After all, surviving in the desert is nothing more than plain old common sense with a few added bells and whistles."[10]
>
> —Felice Prager, writer for DesertUSA

If the worst-case scenario comes to pass, such as if a hiker gets injured, stranded, or lost, the best thing for the person

▲ Desert campers may need to be prepared for both hot daytime temperatures and cold nighttime temperatures. Sleeping bags should be warm enough for the coldest temperatures at the camping site.

involved to do is to try to get help in whatever way possible. Waving around a signal mirror or an emergency blanket, using a satellite phone, writing "SOS" in the sand, or doing some combination of all three can help. Finally, people stuck in the desert must remain calm if at all possible. David Alloway has some advice: "The basics of desert survival? Prepare for the worst. Control panic. Use your brain. Use energy and water wisely. Be ready to signal. Don't listen to your stomach," he writes. "Most of all, do not fear the desert. For many of us, it is home."[11]

ESSENTIAL FACTS

SURVIVAL STORIES

- Claire Nelson is a New Zealand journalist and the author of the memoir *Things I Learned from Falling*. She survived a 25-foot (7.6 m) fall and a shattered pelvis in Joshua Tree National Park in 2018.

- Mauro Prosperi, a police officer and former Olympic pentathlete, took part in the Marathon des Sables in the Moroccan Sahara and got trapped in a sandstorm. He spent nine days wandering around alone in the desert before finding his way back to civilization.

- Donna Cooper, her daughter Gina, and their friend Jenny Leung got stranded in Death Valley in 2010 when their car ran out of gas. They survived by finding an abandoned campsite and waiting for rescue.

- Danelle Ballengee is a two-time world champion in adventure racing and a seven-time Ironman Triathlon finisher who survived a 60-foot (18 m) fall in Moab, Utah. Her dog, Taz, led rescuers to her.

- Tamra McBeath-Riley and Phu Tran, along with Claire Hockridge, became stranded in the Australian outback after their truck got stuck in a riverbed. McBeath-Riley and Tran were rescued, but Hockridge died before rescuers found her.

DESERT SURVIVAL

- Deserts are arid regions. Deserts can be divided into four main types: subtropical, semiarid, coastal, and cold.

- Deserts are found on all seven continents. They cover about one-fifth of Earth's surface and are home to approximately one-sixth of the world's population.

- Some of the main hazards of deserts are dehydration, hypothermia, heatstroke, poisonous plants, venomous animals, sandstorms, and flash floods.

- To survive in a desert, the most important thing to do is to stay hydrated.

- Other survival tips include wearing light-colored, lightweight clothing that covers most of a person's skin, along with wearing sunglasses, a broad-brimmed hat, and closed-toe shoes such as hiking boots.

- The best things to bring in a desert survival kit include a first aid kit, sunscreen, a signal mirror, a loud whistle, an emergency blanket, waterproof matches, and a water-purifying device or tablets.

QUOTE

"You can't live without water, and in a desert environment, you can't count on finding it."

—*Adam Roy,* Backpacker *magazine reporter, 2017*

antiseptic
A preparation that cleans and disinfects to prevent the growth of disease-causing germs.

careen
To move quickly in a random, often out-of-control direction.

evaporate
To turn from liquid into vapor.

hypothermia
The condition of having an unusually low body temperature, which endangers health.

Ironman Triathlon
A long-distance race that consists of a 2.4-mile (3.9 km) swim, a 112-mile (180 km) bicycle ride, and a 26.2-mile (42.2 km) run.

memoir
A type of nonfiction writing that tells a true story about a period in its author's life from the author's perspective.

monolith
A large, upright block of stone, such as a pillar or monument.

pentathlete
An athlete who competes in five sports during one event: fencing, swimming, horse riding, pistol shooting, and running.

phenomenon
An exceptional or unusual event.

prospector
A person who searches for mineral deposits, especially by digging and sifting.

reap
To receive a benefit or reward as a consequence of one's own or other people's actions.

shrine
An area or monument dedicated to a particular religious figure and often containing a statue, image, or object depicting that figure.

stamina
The ability to maintain prolonged physical or mental effort.

strenuous
Requiring great energy or effort.

topographic
Relating to the arrangement of physical features of a landscape, including mountains, hills, and rivers.

tourniquet
A device, such as a piece of cloth, that is wrapped tightly around a leg or an arm to prevent blood loss from a wound.

ADDITIONAL RESOURCES

SELECTED BIBLIOGRAPHY

Alloway, David. *Desert Survival Skills*. University of Texas, 2000.

Jhung, Lisa. "Danelle Ballengee: Five Years Later." *Runners World*, 11 Dec. 2011, runnersworld.com. Accessed 16 Mar. 2023.

Nelson, Claire. *Things I Learned from Falling*. HarperOne, 2021.

Sides, Hampton. "Crazy in the Desert." *Men's Journal*, 4 Dec. 2017, mensjournal.com. Accessed 16 Apr. 2023.

FURTHER READINGS

Hand, Carol. *Climate Scientists*. Abdo, 2020.

Sonneborn, Liz. *Rock and Mountain Survival Stories*. Abdo, 2024.

Towell, Colin. *The Survival Handbook: Essential Skills for Outdoor Adventure*. DK, 2020.

ONLINE RESOURCES

To learn more about the desert and survival, please visit **abdobooklinks.com** or scan this QR code. These links are routinely monitored and updated to provide the most current information available.

MORE INFORMATION

For more information on this subject, contact or visit the following organizations:

DEATH VALLEY NATIONAL PARK
*Airport Rd.
Furnace Creek, CA 92328
nps.gov/deva/planyourvisit/things2do.htm*

The Furnace Creek Visitor Center serves as the entryway to Death Valley National Park. It features informational exhibits, a film about the park, and a gift shop. Tourists can pay the entrance fee, find out about popular trails, learn safety precautions, and talk to park rangers.

JOSHUA TREE NATIONAL PARK VISITOR CENTER
*6533 Freedom Way
Twentynine Palms, CA 92277
joshuatree.org/visitor-centers/joshua-tree-cultural-center.html*

This is the headquarters for Joshua Tree National Park and one of four visitor centers located in the area. Here, travelers can learn about the area through exhibits, buy memorabilia and books at the park store, talk to rangers about hikes and sightseeing adventures, and purchase park passes.

MOAB INFORMATION CENTER
*25 E. Center St.
Moab, UT 84532
discovermoab.com/visitor-center*

This center offers information on recreational opportunities throughout southeastern Utah. There are interpretive displays and a large gift shop that stocks guidebooks, maps, videos, and postcards. Here, travelers can find out about the town and two popular sites, Canyonlands National Park and Arches National Park.

SOURCE NOTES

CHAPTER 1. A TERRIFYING FALL

1. Katherine Gallagher. "10 Extraordinary Joshua Tree National Park Facts." *Treehugger*, 23 Aug. 2021, treehugger.com. Accessed 15 June 2023.
2. "Lost Palms Trail." *AllTrails*, n.d., alltrails.com. Accessed 15 June 2023.
3. "Shenandoah National Park Virginia: How to Determine Hiking Difficulty." *National Park Service*, 5 Dec. 2017, nps.gov. Accessed 15 June 2023.
4. Sherry Barkas. "'I'm Grateful to Be Alive.' New Zealand Hiker Recalls Ordeal at Joshua Tree National Park." *Desert Sun*, 18 July 2018, desertsun.com. Accessed 15 June 2023.
5. Barkas, "'I'm Grateful to Be Alive.'"
6. Maura Fox. "'I Was Going to Die in the Desert.'" *Outside*, 25 June 2021, outsideonline.com. Accessed 15 June 2023.
7. Barkas, "'I'm Grateful to Be Alive.'"
8. Jason Vermes. "What a Harrowing Fall in the Desert Taught Claire Nelson about Life and Regrets." *CBC*, 9 July 2021, cbc.ca. Accessed 15 June 2023.
9. Barkas, "'I'm Grateful to Be Alive.'"
10. Barkas, "'I'm Grateful to Be Alive.'"
11. Vermes, "Harrowing Fall in the Desert."
12. Danelle Ballengee. "Experience: I Fell Down a Canyon." *Guardian*, 2 Dec. 2016, theguardian.com. Accessed 15 June 2023.
13. David Alloway. "Desert Survival Skills: How to Survive in the Desert." *DesertUSA*, n.d., desertusa.com. Accessed 15 June 2023.
14. Alloway, "Desert Survival Skills."

CHAPTER 2. THE DANGERS OF THE DESERT

1. "Desert." *National Geographic Education*, 1 May 2023, education.nationalgeographic.org. Accessed 15 June 2023.
2. "Desert."
3. "The Desert Biome." *UC Museum of Paleontology*, 1996, ucmp.berkeley.edu. Accessed 15 June 2023.
4. "Desert."
5. "The Desert Biome."
6. Alisa Mala. "The Arabian Desert." *World Atlas*, 3 Dec. 2020, worldatlas.com. Accessed 15 June 2023.
7. Nathaniel Whelan. "The 10 Largest Deserts in the World." *World Atlas*, 14 Feb. 2023, worldatlas.com. Accessed 15 June 2023.
8. Nathaniel Whelan. "Types of Deserts." *World Atlas*, 23 Oct. 2020, worldatlas.com. Accessed 15 June 2023.
9. "The Desert Biome."
10. "Ranking of the Largest Deserts on Earth (In Million Square Miles)." *Statista*, 22 Jan. 2016, statista.com. Accessed 15 June 2023.
11. Whelan, "Types of Deserts."
12. "Hypothermia." *Mayo Clinic*, 5 Mar. 2022, mayoclinic.org. Accessed 15 June 2023.
13. Adam Roy. "4 Desert Dangers and How to Survive Them." *Backpacker*, 25 Aug. 2017, backpacker.com. Accessed 15 June 2023.
14. "Heatstroke." *Mayo Clinic*, 25 June 2022, mayoclinic.org. Accessed 15 June 2023.
15. Juana Summers, Vincent Acovino, and Christopher Intagliata. "What Extreme Heat Means for Our Long Term Health." *NPR*, 21 July 2022, npr.org. Accessed 15 June 2023.

16. "Grand Canyon National Park Arizona: Lightning Danger." *National Park Service*, 3 Aug. 2018, nps.gov. Accessed 15 June 2023.

17. Susan Strom. "Chasing the Desert Lightning: Getting the Picture." *DesertUSA*, n.d., desertusa.com. Accessed 15 June 2023.

CHAPTER 3. CLAIRE IS FOUND

1. Rose George. "*Things I Learned from Falling* Review—Desert Hike, Accident, No Hope of Rescue." *Guardian*, 11 Mar. 2020, theguardian.com. Accessed 15 June 2023.

2. Jacob Adelman. "Hiker Followed Shade during 6 Days in Desert." *NBC News*, 5 Oct. 2010, nbcnews.com. Accessed 15 June 2023.

3. Maura Fox. "'I Was Going to Die in the Desert.'" *Outside*, 25 June 2021, outsideonline.com. Accessed 15 June 2023.

4. Jason Vermes. "What a Harrowing Fall in the Desert Taught Claire Nelson about Life and Regrets." *CBC*, 9 July 2021, cbc.ca. Accessed 15 June 2023.

5. Sherry Barkas. "'I'm Grateful to Be Alive.' New Zealand Hiker Recalls Ordeal at Joshua Tree National Park." *Desert Sun*, 18 July 2018, desertsun.com. Accessed 15 June 2023.

6. Vermes, "Harrowing Fall in the Desert."

7. Fox, "'I Was Going to Die in the Desert.'"

8. Vermes, "Harrowing Fall in the Desert."

9. Vermes, "Harrowing Fall in the Desert."

10. "Ladyeclaire." *Instagram*, 21 Jan. 2019, instagram.com. Accessed 15 June 2023.

CHAPTER 4. THE RACE TO NOWHERE

1. Michael Anderson. "5 Largest Deserts in the World." *GeoJango Maps*, 21 May 2021, geojango.com. Accessed 15 June 2023.

2. "Interesting Facts about the Sahara Desert." *Global Adventure Challenges*, n.d., globaladventurechallenges.com. Accessed 15 June 2023.

3. "Home Page." *Marathon des Sables*, n.d., marathondessables.co.uk. Accessed 15 June 2023.

4. "Home Page."

5. Hampton Sides. "Crazy in the Desert." *Men's Journal*, 4 Dec. 2017, mensjournal.com. Accessed 15 June 2023.

6. Mauro Prosperi. "How I Drank Urine and Bat Blood to Survive." *BBC News*, 27 Nov. 2014, bbc.com. Accessed 15 June 2023.

7. Sides, "Crazy in the Desert."

8. Sides, "Crazy in the Desert."

9. Sides, "Crazy in the Desert."

10. Sides, "Crazy in the Desert."

11. Sides, "Crazy in the Desert."

12. Sides, "Crazy in the Desert."

13. Sides, "Crazy in the Desert."

14. Patrick McCarthy. "Alone in the Sahara: The Survival Story of Mauro Prosperi." *Recoil Offgrid*, 8 Apr. 2018, offgridweb.com. Accessed 15 June 2023.

SOURCE NOTES CONTINUED

CHAPTER 5. A ROAD TRIP GONE WRONG

1. Kenneth Miller. "Survival Stories: Hot, Thirsty, and Lost in Death Valley." *Reader's Digest*, 28 Mar. 2022, rd.com. Accessed 15 June 2023.
2. "Death Valley National Park: Summer Visitor Guide." *National Park Service*, n.d., nps.gov. Accessed 15 June 2023.
3. Miller, "Survival Stories."
4. Tom Knudson. "In Death Valley, Don't Depend on GPS or Phone." *Daily Press*, 21 Feb. 2011, vvdailypress.com. Accessed 15 June 2023.
5. Knudson, "In Death Valley, Don't Depend on GPS or Phone."
6. Miller, "Survival Stories."
7. "Lost in Death Valley: One Family's Horrifying Experience." *ABC News*, 6 Jan. 2023, abcnews.go.com. Accessed 15 June 2023.
8. Miller, "Survival Stories."
9. Miller, "Survival Stories."
10. "Ecology of Death Valley National Park." *US Geological Survey*, n.d., usgs.gov. Accessed 15 June 2023.
11. "Lost in Death Valley."
12. "Lost in Death Valley."

CHAPTER 6. TAZ TO THE RESCUE

1. Brian Metzler. "Between a Dog and a Hard Place." *Bark*, Aug. 2022, thebark.com. Accessed 15 June 2023.
2. Metzler, "Between a Dog and a Hard Place."
3. Danelle Ballengee. "Experience: I Fell Down a Canyon." *Guardian*, 2 Dec. 2016, theguardian.com. Accessed 15 June 2023.
4. "Arches National Park Utah: Delicate Arch." *National Park Service*, 10 July 2021, nps.gov. Accessed 15 June 2023.
5. "Moab, UT, December 2023." *AccuWeather*, n.d., accuweather.com. Accessed 15 June 2023.
6. Phillip Gary Smith. "Screams of Pain: The Danelle Ballengee Story." *Snowshoe Magazine*, 12 Aug. 2021, snowshoemag.com. Accessed 15 June 2023.
7. Smith, "Screams of Pain."
8. Metzler, "Between a Dog and a Hard Place."
9. Metzler, "Between a Dog and a Hard Place."
10. Thom Patterson. "The Mysterious Science behind Lifesaving Dogs." *CNN*, 10 July 2018, cnn.com. Accessed 15 June 2023.
11. Metzler, "Between a Dog and a Hard Place."
12. Smith, "Screams of Pain."
13. Metzler, "Between a Dog and a Hard Place."
14. Lisa Jhung. "Danelle Ballengee: Five Years Later." *Runner's World*, 11 Dec. 2011, runnersworld.com. Accessed 15 June 2023.

CHAPTER 7. TRAPPED IN THE OUTBACK

1. Emily Smith. "Remote Australia Deaths Prompts Warning Outback Travel Dangers Could Rise." *ABC News*, 8 Nov. 2018, abc.net.au. Accessed 15 June 2023.
2. Connor Sephton. "Australia: Outback Survivor's Fears for Partner and Friend Missing in Searing Heat." *Sky News*, 2 Dec. 2019, news.sky.com. Accessed 15 June 2023.
3. Lauren Roberts and Samantha Jonscher. "Tamra McBeath-Riley Describes Fight for Survival during 12 Days Lost in NT Outback." *ABC News*, 1 Dec. 2019, abc.net.au. Accessed 15 June 2023.
4. "How to Get Your Car Unstuck from the Mud." *Les Schwab Tire Center*, n.d., lesschwab.com. Accessed 15 June 2023.

5. Isabella Kwai. "'Incredible Story of Survival': Woman Rescued after 12 Days in Outback." *New York Times*, 2 Dec. 2019, nytimes.com. Accessed 15 June 2023.

6. "Guide to Uluru and Kata Tjuta." *Tourism Australia*, n.d., australia.com. Accessed 15 June 2023.

7. "Kata Tjuta." *Parks Australia*, n.d., parksaustralia.gov.au. Accessed 15 June 2023.

8. Samantha Jonscher. "South Australian Man Phu Tran Found Alive by Pastoralist after Almost Two Weeks Missing in NT Outback." *ABC News*, 3 Dec. 2019, abc.net.au. Accessed 15 June 2023.

9. Rob Picheta and Joshua Berlinger. "Body Found in Search for Woman Missing in Australian Outback." *CNN*, 4 Dec. 2019, cnn.com. Accessed 15 June 2023.

10. Jon Haworth. "Man Miraculously Found after Being Lost in the Australian Outback for 2 Weeks." *Good Morning America*, 23 Dec. 2020, goodmorningamerica.com. Accessed 15 June 2023.

CHAPTER 8. SURVIVING THE DESERT

1. David Alloway. "Desert Survival Skills: How to Survive in the Desert." *DesertUSA*, n.d., desertusa.com. Accessed 15 June 2023.

2. Adam Roy. "4 Desert Dangers and How to Survive Them." *Backpacker*, 25 Aug. 2017, backpacker.com. Accessed 15 June 2023.

3. Alloway, "Desert Survival Skills."

4. "Desert Hiking Clothing—What to Wear and Why." *Trek Southwest*, n.d., treksw.com. Accessed 15 June 2023.

5. "Sunscreen FAQs." *American Academy of Dermatology Association*, 17 Feb. 2023, aad.org. Accessed 15 June 2023.

6. Annemarie K. "Sun Protection Tips for Summer Adventures in the Desert." *REI Co-op*, May 2014, destinations.rei.com. Accessed 15 June 2023.

7. "LifeStraw Personal Water Filter." *LifeStraw*, n.d., lifestraw.com. Accessed 15 June 2023.

8. Felice Prager. "26 Tips for Surviving in the Desert: The Desert Can Be an Unforgiving Place." *DesertUSA*, n.d., desertusa.com. Accessed 15 June 2023.

9. "Desert Safety Tips and Desert Survival." *DesertUSA*, n.d., desertusa.com. Accessed 15 June 2023.

10. Prager, "26 Tips for Surviving in the Desert."

11. Alloway, "Desert Survival Skills."

INDEX

Alice Springs, Australia, 81
Alley, Micah, 54
Alloway, David, 15, 85, 86, 99
Amasa Back Trail, 63, 70
animals, 17–18, 20–22, 26, 29, 39, 44, 56, 64
    dogs, 14, 64, 67, 70–72, 76, 79–80
    snakes, 20–21, 26, 64
Antarctic desert, 18, 19, 21
Arabian Desert, 19
Arctic desert, 19, 21
Atacama Desert, 13, 21

backpacks, 88, 89, 91
Ballengee, Danelle, 14, 63–72, 73
biking, 86

Callagan, Charlie, 53, 54
camping, 5, 76–77, 98
canyons, 10, 14, 30, 65, 68, 73, 81, 98
    Grand Canyon, 25, 27
Chihuahuan Desert, 19
coastal deserts, 18, 21
cold deserts, 18, 21–22
compasses, 42, 80, 91
Cooper, Donna, 14, 51–61
Cooper, Gina, 51, 53, 55

Death Valley, 6, 14, 51–53, 54, 56, 61
    Scotty's Castle, 52, 55, 57–58

dehydration, 8, 23–24, 30, 34, 41, 43, 57, 76, 81, 86, 88

fences, 82–83
first aid kits, 55, 89, 92
food, 12, 15, 29–30, 42, 44, 55, 57, 67, 73, 76, 79, 82, 89, 91

Gobi Desert, 19
GPS, 27, 53, 54, 55, 61, 80, 89, 94
Great Basin, 19

hats, 6, 31, 88, 89
hiking, 5–9, 12, 14, 30, 35–37, 63, 67, 76, 81, 82, 85–86, 88, 91, 94, 95, 98
Hockridge, Claire, 76, 79, 81–83
hypothermia, 23, 66, 72, 91

I Shouldn't Be Alive, 73

Joshua Tree National Park, 6–8, 12, 14, 29, 30, 35, 37

Leung, Jenny, 51, 57, 61

maps, 8, 31, 42, 53, 54, 61, 89, 94, 97
Marathon des Sables, 14, 40
McBeath-Riley, Tamra, 76–83

110

mirages, 27
Moab, Utah, 14, 64–65, 68–72, 73
Mojave Desert, 6, 19, 27

Nelson, Claire, 5–12, 14, 29–37

oases, 8–9, 27, 35, 37, 86
outback, 15, 75–76, 78, 81, 82

park rangers, 9, 14, 53, 54, 61, 95
plants, 6, 17–22, 25–26, 27, 39, 64, 75, 78, 81
  cacti, 20, 56, 57
pocketknives, 42, 89, 91
Prosperi, Mauro, 14, 40–49

rivers, 27, 65, 75, 78, 80
Rosenthal, Ed, 30

Sahara Desert, 12, 14, 18, 19, 27, 39–40, 43, 48
search and rescue, 14, 36, 42, 54, 61, 70–71, 79, 80–83, 91, 95
semiarid deserts, 18, 20–21, 42
shade, 15, 27, 78, 90
shoes, 88, 89
Sonoran Desert, 19
SOS, 43, 94, 95, 99
subtropical deserts, 18–20
sunburn, 24, 31, 90

sunglasses, 88, 89
sunscreen, 6, 89, 90–91
sweat, 15, 23, 65, 73

temperatures, 12–13, 18, 21–24, 29, 39, 43, 51–53, 55, 56, 65–66, 72, 76, 88
tires, 78, 81
trail-rating systems, 9
Tran, Phu, 76, 79, 81–83
Tuareg, 48

urine, 23, 32–33, 34, 42

water, 8, 10, 12–13, 15, 17–18, 21, 23, 26–27, 29, 30, 32–33, 40–43, 47, 55, 56, 57, 65, 76, 78–82, 83, 86, 89, 99
  filters, 92, 94
  purification tablets, 92
weather, 24–26, 98
  floods, 25–26, 98
  lightning, 25–26, 98
  precipitation, 17, 20, 22, 23, 25, 39, 52, 98
  sandstorms, 14, 24, 41, 42

ABOUT THE AUTHOR

ALEXIS BURLING

Alexis Burling has written dozens of articles and books for young readers on a variety of topics ranging from current events and biographies of famous people to nutrition, fitness, careers, and money management. She is also a professional book critic with reviews of adult and young adult books, author interviews, and other publishing industry–related articles published in the *New York Times, Washington Post Book World, San Francisco Chronicle*, and more. Alexis has had the pleasure of hiking and backpacking in many beautiful deserts in the world, including Death Valley National Park, Joshua Tree National Park, and Chile's Atacama Desert. Thankfully she was prepared and didn't get lost. She lives in White Salmon, Washington, with her husband and cats.